Birding Maine

Over 90 Prime Birding Sites at 40 Locations

Tom Seymour

FALCON GUIDES ®

GUILFORD, CONNECTICUT
HELENA, MONTANA
AN IMPRINT OF THE GLOBE PEQUOT PRESS

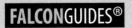

Falcon and FalconGuides are registered trademarks of
Morris Book Publishing, LLC.

Text design by Eileen Hine
Maps created by Melissa Baker © Morris Book
    Publishing, LLC
Photos by Tom Seymour

Library of Congress Cataloging-in-Publication Data
  is available.
ISBN 978-0-7627-4224-0

Printed in the United States of America
10 9 8 7 6 5 4 3 2 1

To buy books in quantity for corporate use
or incentives, call **(800) 962–0973**
or e-mail **premiums@GlobePequot.com.**

The author and The Globe Pequot Press assume no liability for accidents happening to,
or injuries sustained by, readers who engage in the activities described in this book.

Contents

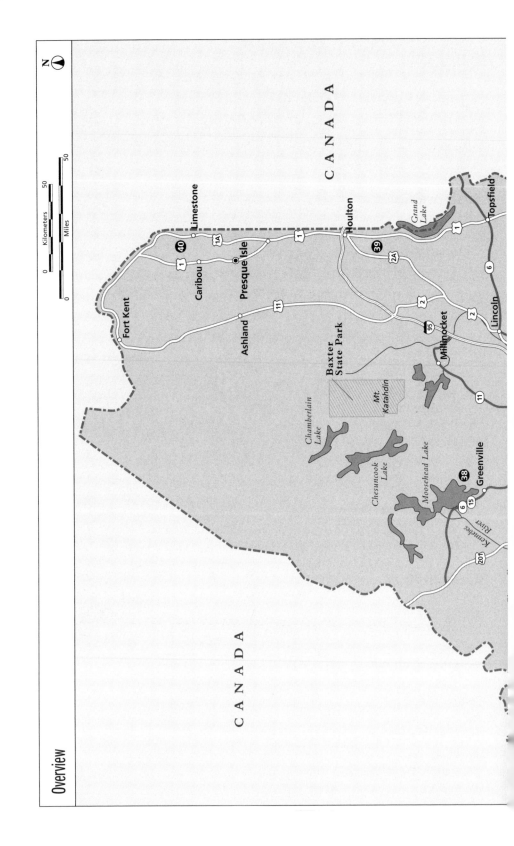

Overview

N

CANADA

Fort Kent

Limestone

1

40

Caribou

1A

Ashland

Presque Isle

11

Baxter
State Park

Chamberlain
Lake

Mt.
Katahdin

1

Houlton

2A

39

6

1

Topsfield

Chesuncook
Lake

95

Millinocket

2

Lincoln

Moosehead Lake

2

11

Grand
Lake

Greenville

38

6

15

Kennebec
River

201

CANADA

Kilometers
0   50

Miles
0   50

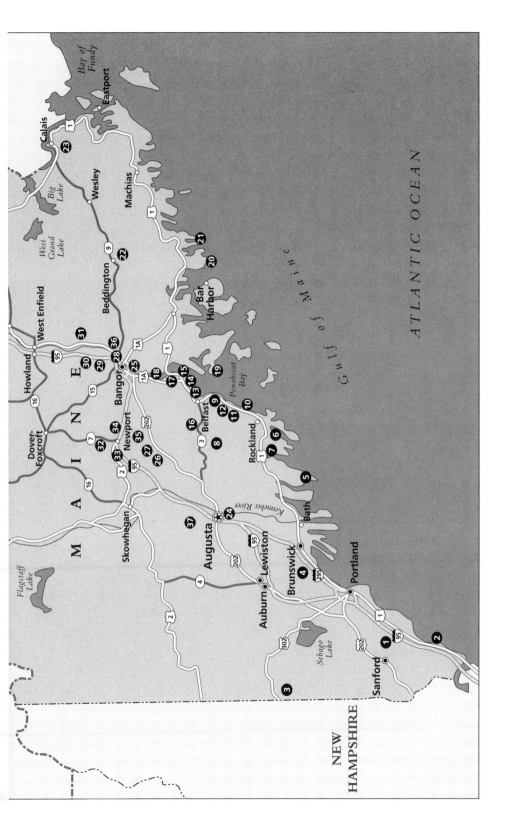

Northern Maine

Preface

When Globe Pequot acquisition editor Bill Schneider suggested I write a birding guide for Maine, I was thrilled. Schneider lives in the West, though, and to him, Maine is a small state. Given that, I was directed to prepare a small book, with only 25 or 30 sites. This presented a problem, since Maine has hundreds of prime birding sites. Then Schneider went on to say that I was to include lots of side information such as nearby places of interest, as well as other nearby birding sites. This put a new perspective on things.

Maine has the distinction of being about 90 percent forested. Add to that a diverse geography, including many miles of pristine shoreline on the Atlantic Ocean, lakes, ponds, marshes, rivers, streams, high mountains, fields and open, rolling hills. Birding in Maine involves getting out in nature, in the most remote, wild and beautiful state in the northeast United States. Admittedly, some birders, anxious to add new conquests to their life lists, frequent wastewater treatment plants and other, less-than-pristine locations. It is not within the scope of this book to direct people to such sites.

I have included not only some of Maine's more famous and renowned birding sites, but also lots of newly discovered sites. Many of these are so new that the birding potential is still being explored. Birders visiting these sites can assure themselves that they are participating in something important, namely, acting as birding pioneers. Few eastern states can make such a boast.

All the sites in this book are not only excellent places for birding, but also great places to visit for their own sake. Many of these are ideally suited for families with children. Most of the sites included here are publicly owned, or are owned by nonprofit organizations that allow public access. Finally, all the sites are set amidst some of Maine's more beautiful, and interesting scenery.

The number of people looking to birding as a pastime has grown dramatically over the last few years. In addition to writing outdoor articles for magazines, as well as field guides such as this, I write several columns for my local, weekly newspaper. One of these includes a regular feature called "Under the Feeder." Here, I not only share with readers notes about what birds I have seen during the previous week, but readers contact me and tell me of their sightings. The thing has become enormously popular, and is a pretty good indicator of the growing interest in the backyard bird feeder and birding in general.

When people ask me where is the best place to go bird watching, I always tell them to concentrate upon their own backyard. Now, with the advent of *Birding Maine,* I can add all the sites mentioned in this book.

Acknowledgments

Thanks to The Globe Pequot Press acquisition editor Bill Schneider for suggesting and assigning this project to me.

Special thanks go to Tom Hodgeman, wildlife biologist with the Maine Department of Inland Fisheries and Wildlife. Tom's technical assistance and suggestions were invaluable. Thanks also to Thomas Schaeffer and Richard Bard, both of the Maine Department of Inland Fisheries and Wildlife Region C office, for providing a wealth of information on birding opportunities in wildlife management areas in Down East Maine.

Dan Avener suggested sites, helped identify bird species present, and inspired confidence. Ken Allen, associate editor of *Maine Sportsman* magazine, and Harry Vanderweide, editor of *Maine Sportsman,* both assisted in suggesting sites and noting bird species.

And finally, special thanks to all the people from countless managing agencies who kindly provided help and background material and who in general went out of their way to assist me.

Introduction

Maine enjoys several impressive distinctions. It is the only state to share a border with just one other state. New Hampshire, Vermont, Connecticut, and Rhode Island could fit into Maine, with plenty of room to spare. Maine is approximately 90 percent forested. Approximately one-tenth of Maine's 33,215 square miles is water. And in between the forest and the sea are mountains, lakes, parks, wetlands, alder-filled uplands, impoundments, and fields—all places where birders congregate to pursue their interests.

Maine is a state of contrasts. It sits far enough to the north that it represents the northernmost extent of many plants, animals, and birds. At the same time, Maine is the southern foothold for many northern species. The jet stream usually passes through or close by Maine, and fierce storms often carry with them many accidentals—birds that do not live in Maine but arrive here purely by accident.

Each of Maine's four seasons is distinct and separate. Winter, especially in northern and central areas, is often fierce, with deep snow and prolonged subzero temperatures. Summer is best described as temperate, but heat spells can and do drive Mainers to the nearest lake, pond, or beach. Spring and fall see migrating birds of all sorts. In spring great waves of migrating warblers draw people to coastal areas to witness this awe-inspiring event. Fall brings the annual hawk migration. Hawks flying south from far northern Maine and the Canadian provinces to the north pass through the Maine coast, following the contour of the shoreline, which includes coastal mountains. Early-morning vigils atop such noted peaks as Cadillac Mountain and Mount Battie reward participants with close-up views of their favorite birds of prey.

Maine's bays and onshore ocean areas host a great variety of waterfowl, especially in winter. And in summer birders can view shorebirds and ocean birds. While a boat trip is the easiest way to see ocean birds, they also can be seen from shore at a variety of locations, many of which are listed in this book.

Maine Specialties

Far northern Maine is home to several species that are rarely seen farther south, such as the Gray Jay and Spruce Grouse. Both these birds are at home in wilderness settings and have little fear of humans. The Gray Jay figures prominently in Maine folklore and legend, probably because of its habit of following old-time woods workers to their camps and eating the stale biscuits and breads left out for them.

The coast of Maine has its own special birds, and none among them draws more attention than the Atlantic Puffin. Some birders visit Maine specifically to see their first puffin. Atlantic Puffin are one of three North American puffin species and the only one to occur on the east coast. Puffins—black-and-white

Atlantic Puffin nest on Maine's offshore islands, beginning in April and continuing through August. Then Atlantic Puffin move out to sea, where they remain until the following spring. Powerful swimmers, Atlantic Puffin can dive to depths of 100 feet. Fish are Atlantic Puffin's mainstay, but they also eat aquatic insects.

Fortunately for visitors to Maine, a number of commercial ventures feature regularly scheduled "puffin cruises." These are the best way to get a good, relatively close-up view of puffins on their offshore islands. But before setting out on a cruise, a visit to the Puffin Project Visitor Center (PPVC) is recommended. Located at 311 Main Street (U.S. Route 1) in Rockland, PPVC features interactive exhibits and real-time video cam images and sounds of puffins as well as other seabirds. The "Puffin Cam" is located on Seal Island National Wildlife Refuge, an offshore island in the Gulf of Maine. PPVC also features maps and exhibits describing the Audubon Society's conservation efforts on Maine's offshore seabird islands.

Visitors to PPVC can also watch the 20-minute film *Project Puffin,* which highlights puffin and other seabird restoration efforts along the Maine coast. Additionally, PPVC provides visitors with boat schedules to the seabird islands. Admission to the visitor center is free. To contact PPVC, call (207) 596-5566 or (877) 4-PUFFIN, or visit www.projectpuffin.org. A visit to the Web site will help you to learn more about Project Puffin as you watch images from the Seal Island Puffin Cam.

Here are some contracts to help you book your own puffin cruise.

Cap'n Fish sails from Pier 1 in Boothbay Harbor to Eastern Egg Rock. Call (800) 636-3244, or visit www.capnfishmotel.com/boattrips.htm. Cap'n Fish runs from mid-June through late August.

Hardy Boat Cruises leave Shaw's Wharf in New Harbor for Eastern Egg Rock. Call (800) 2-PUFFIN or (207) 677-2026, or visit www.hardyboat.com. Hardy Boat Cruises run from early June through late August.

Monhegan Boat Line offers a puffin/nature cruise to Eastern Egg Rock from Port Clyde. These run from late June through mid-August. Call (207) 372-8848; write to Monhegan Boat Line, P.O. Box 238, Port Clyde, ME 04855; or e-mail: barstow@monheganboat.com.

Come Prepared

Whenever you visit Maine, and wherever you go, remember that temperatures can drop sharply and without much notice. This is especially important to consider when going out on or near the fresh or salt water. Summertime temperatures may range up into the mid-90s inland, but out at sea conditions may be brisk. Always bring a sweater, sweatshirt, or windbreaker. A water-resistant poncho is invaluable. Also, headgear is a must, not only for protection from the sun but also to help thwart biting insects.

Speaking of insects, Maine has its share of pesky nuisances. Mosquitoes are

Red-breasted Nuthatch

ubiquitous, and blackflies, tiny biting gnats, hatch out in great swarms from early spring right through summer. In summer, savage deerflies seek human necks and ears. Ticks, once a problem for other states to the south of Maine, are now present in numbers and carry the threat of Lyme disease. Even while on a boat at sea, you may suffer from attacks by biting insects. Long sleeves, long pants, and an insect repellent containing DEET are your best defenses against biting insects.

Wildlife

Maine has the largest black bear population in the continental United States. The bulk of Maine's bear population resides in northern Maine, with a substantial number in eastern Maine. However, while other parts of the state have few year-round bears, every county in Maine has visiting bears at one time or another. In late summer and fall, in an effort to consume as many calories as possible prior to hibernating, male black bears will range up to 100 miles in search of food. Since blueberries are a favorite staple for bears, this means that bears can be present in any blueberry land in Maine.

In spring bears leave their winter dens and, famished with hunger, go searching for anything and everything edible. At this time bears are cranky—if you see a bear, do not approach it. Females with cubs are especially bad tempered. Stay as far away as possible.

That said, bears tend to be shy and reclusive and will do their best to avoid a confrontation with a human. Leave them alone, and they will leave you alone.

Moose, probably the most famed of all Maine's big-game animals, are ubiquitous in northern and eastern Maine and are increasing their population throughout the rest of the state. Many sites in this book are located in some of Maine's finest moose territory. Like black bears, moose will avoid you if possible. However, moose are never to be approached. A cow moose with her calf will chase an intruder. A bull moose can be ornery for no particular reason. Both are to be treated with great respect—and from a safe distance. To avoid an encounter with a 1,000-pound living tank with antlers, do not ever approach a moose. Do, however, carry a camera and be prepared to take as many photos as you can of these giant symbols of our greatest eastern wilderness.

Mountain lion, or cougar, sightings have become commonplace. Yet mountain lions are not officially recognized as having established a breeding population in Maine.

Gray wolves sometimes filter into Maine from Canada, but these, too, are not official residents. Neither cougars nor wolves are of much concern to anyone recreating in the Maine wilds. Another creature, though, is present in every county, filling the nighttime air with its howling. The eastern coyote, a relatively new animal to Maine, is one of the state's major predators. While few documented cases of coyote attacks exist, coyotes are not afraid of humans and should be assiduously avoided.

Bobcats and Canada lynx are both present in Maine. Neither poses any threat to humans. In fact, it is a rare treat to see either one of these feline predators.

Smaller mammals such as red foxes and raccoons are present throughout Maine. While they are not normally belligerent, they command respect because they are potential rabies carriers. Every so often, rabies sweep through Maine, and all warm-blooded animals are subject to its ravages. Humans can easily avoid confrontations with rabid animals by avoiding all contact with wild animals. In fact, the bottom line regarding all Maine mammals is this: Do not approach any wild animal. If you see an animal that shows signs of sickness or acts strangely, leave the area immediately and contact the nearest authorities.

Finally, Maine has no poisonous snakes. You can walk, hike, and climb to your heart's content without fear of an encounter with a poisonous reptile.

Water

In the author's youth, springs, remote ponds, and mountain streams were presumed to contain safe drinking water. That no longer holds true. Never drink from a stream or any other open source of water. A few roadside springs still remain, where locals get fresh, free springwater. These are no longer marked as such, though, because of liability concerns. It is best to carry your own water wherever you go.

Endangered Species Listing

Maine established its endangered and threatened species act in 1975. At that time only federally listed species were included, but over the years many more species were added. Today ten bird species are listed as endangered and five are on the threatened list. The Maine Endangered Species Act addresses only animals that are in danger of disappearing from Maine. To qualify for inclusion on the list, a species must be wild, native to Maine, and spend a portion of its annual life cycle in the state. The list is broken down into four categories: endangered, threatened, of special concern, and extirpated. The two last categories are used for planning and informational purposes only.

The task of monitoring these species is entrusted to the Maine Wildlife Resource Assessment Section and the Wildlife Management section of Maine's Department of Inland Fisheries and Wildlife (DIF&W). Individual species accounts are available from DIF&W as printable pdf files. To obtain these visit the DIF&W Web site at www.state.me.us/ifw/wildlife/etweb/specieslist.htm.

The following birds are on Maine's endangered and threatened species lists:

Rose-breasted Grosbeak

Maine Endangered Species

Golden Eagle *(Aquila chrysaetos)*
Peregrine Falcon *(Falco peregrinus)*
Piping Plover *(Charadrius melodus)*
Roseate Tern *(Sterna dougallii)*
Least Tern *(Sterna antillarum)*
Black Tern *(Chlidonias niger)*
Sedge Wren *(Cistothorus platensis)*
American Pipit *(Anthus rubescens)* (breeding population only)
Grasshopper Sparrow *(Ammodramus savannarum)*
Least Bittern *(Ixobrychus exilis)* (added in 2007)

Maine Threatened Species

Razorbill *(Alca torda)*
Atlantic Puffin *(Fratercula arctica)*
Harlequin Duck *(Histrionicus histrionicus)*
Arctic Tern *(Sterna paradisaea)*
Upland Sandpiper *(Bartramia longicauda)*

Added in 2007 to Threatened Species List:

Barrow's Goldeneye *(Bucephala islandica)*
Black-crowned Night-Heron *(Nycticorax nicticorax)*
Common Moorhen *(Gallinula chloropus)*
Great Cormorant *(Phalacrocorax carbo)*
Short-eared Owl *(Asio flammeus)*

Concerning Maine's endangered and threatened species, a few specifics are in order. First, a pair of Golden Eagle nested in Piscataquis County from 1985 through 1998—the only known breeding pair in the northeastern United States. The site is documented as occupied by nesting Golden Eagle since 1736.

Sadly, there is no evidence of Golden Eagle nesting in Maine since 1999. Golden Eagle are sometimes seen in Maine, though. These may be visitors from Quebec, Canada, or possibly native Maine eagles whose eyries remain undiscovered.

Bald Eagle, though, are prospering in Maine, as elsewhere in the country. Progress in Bald Eagle recovery has inspired state and federal agencies to discuss delisting them. Many sites in this book are prime places to see a Bald Eagle.

The Peregrine Falcon populations in Maine are closely monitored. Falcon numbers in Maine can fluctuate from year to year, which is not attributed to residual contaminants—a good sign. Ongoing restoration efforts hopefully will secure the continuation of this species in Maine.

Grasshopper Sparrow are at the northeastern edge of their range in Maine. During the past 20 years, Grasshopper Sparrow have nested at only four Maine locations. The largest nesting population is located at Kennebunk Plains, one of the sites listed in this book.

Piping Plover, rare in Maine, nest on sandy beaches and sand dunes. Threats to nesting plovers from humans and animals are a perennial concern. However, the good news is that Piping Plover productivity in Maine is among the highest of any place along the Atlantic coast.

Least Tern are at risk similar to the Piping Plover. Human and animal predation threatens nesting terns, and coastal development resulting in habitat loss is an ever-present threat.

Black Tern nest in freshwater wetlands rather than coastal settings. These were once presumed to be fairly common. However, a 1991 statewide census conducted by students of Nokomis High School in Newport indicated that the Black Tern is actually very rare in Maine. DIF&W monitors Black Tern and works to protect tern habitat. Several of the sites listed here host breeding populations.

Harlequin Duck were listed as threatened in 1997 by DIF&W. Since then, the Harlequin Duck population has grown. This trend has also been noted in neighboring New Brunswick and Nova Scotia, Canada. Harlequin Duck may be viewed from some of the sites in this book.

Today's population of Roseate Tern in Maine is significantly fewer than the 200 to 300 pairs noted almost 80 years ago. Roseate Tern nest on Maine's coastal islands, and competition from gulls—predators as well as competitors—along with human disturbance, caused a severe decline in Roseate Tern numbers. Concentrated management, including tern restoration projects, has brought about an increase in numbers. Other terns and seabirds benefit from these efforts as well.

Maine Owls

Owls are perhaps the least understood birds in Maine. Distribution, trends, and abundance of some owl species are unclear. Because of this, Maine Audubon and the Maine Department of Inland Fisheries and Wildlife work jointly to conduct an owl-monitoring program. This relies upon volunteers—persons willing to travel a predetermined route at night, play prerecorded owl calls, and note whether these elicit a response.

Being an owl monitor is not to be taken lightly. In 2007 routes were run between 1:00 and 5:00 a.m. (because of the new start date of daylight saving time), when most people are sleeping. Volunteers are trained to recognize owl calls prior to going on their monitoring route. Also, volunteers are urged to contact local law enforcement authorities to alert them as to date, time, and place of owl-monitoring activity. Signs saying OWL MONITORING SURVEY IN PROGRESS. PLEASE DO NOT DISTURB are placed on the windshield and rear window of survey vehicles.

Protocol for each site involves playing either a CD or a cassette tape that has silent, or passive, times interspersed with owl calls. During the passive times, the volunteer listens for owl replies. Time, wind speed, and temperature are noted in addition to owl response.

Maine is the first state to implement such a project. As a result of Maine's efforts, though, other New England states have begun owl survey programs.

Data collected from these surveys adds considerably to the body of knowledge regarding owls in Maine. For instance, data indicates that Northern Saw-whet Owl, Barred Owl, and Great Horned Owl are distributed statewide. Additionally, some rare species were detected, albeit in limited numbers, including Eastern Screech Owl, Long-eared Owl, and Short-eared Owl.

Owl monitoring efforts show that Barred Owl are the most common owl in Maine, followed by Northern Saw-whet Owl and Great Horned Owl. Long-eared Owl, rare in Maine, are listed as a species of special concern in Maine.

In summary, these volunteer surveys are of great value to biologists. They provide data that can help fill in the gaps regarding owl populations in Maine and, it is hoped, will provide information to indicate whether owl populations in Maine are declining. Much is owed to all those individuals who freely give up a night of sleep to drive around snowy roads in winter and listen for owls.

Birders with Special Needs

Some of the sites listed in this book are set up for persons with special needs. Wheelchair-accessible trails, complete with self-guided and guided nature tours, enable people who have difficulty walking or are in wheelchairs to have a high-quality birding experience. Additionally, many of the sites here, while not wheelchair accessible, can be birded from a motor vehicle. The following sites in this book have provisions for persons with special needs:

Rachel Carson National Wildlife Refuge (Kennebunk Plains listing) has a 1.0-mile wheelchair-accessible gravel path.

Wolfe's Neck State Park (Bradbury Mountain State Park listing) has a 0.5-mile barrier-free path.

Marginal Way has a 1.25-mile wheelchair-accessible path along the ocean.

The Belfast Footbridge over the Passagassawakeag River is wheelchair accessible.

The hiking trail at **Sandy Point Beach** (Sandy Point Wildlife Management Area listing) has a wheelchair-accessible section.

Moosehorn National Wildlife Refuge has two wheelchair-accessible observation decks, as well as the wheelchair-accessible Woodcock Trail, a self-interpreting trail.

Orono Bog Boardwalk is a 1.0-mile wheelchair-accessible boardwalk with benches every 200 feet and numerous interpretative signs at key points.

Wildlife Management Areas

Wildlife Management Areas (WMAs) are state-owned parcels, administered and managed by the Maine Department of Inland Fisheries and Wildlife (DIF&W). These are open to the public, although few are "improved" in any way. Recreational uses at WMAs include hiking, fishing, hunting, and birding, among other activities. Maine's upland game hunting season begins on October 1, and open-firearms season on white-tailed deer runs through November, with a special muzzle-loading season running into the second week of December. It is advised that visitors walking through the woods in any WMA during hunting season wear one, preferably two, items of "blaze-orange" clothing.

Maine has less publicly owned land than other northeastern states; consequently, WMAs are a real treasure. Oddly, these natural areas are not heavily visited. Many are in a completely wild state, and many are prime birding sites. DIF&W maintains a list of WMAs as well as the uses permitted on each WMA. This list is available online at www.mefishwildlife.com.

How to Use This Guide

For purposes of this guide, Maine is divided into five sections: Southern Maine, Midcoast Maine, Down East Maine, Central Maine, and Northern Maine. The sites listed easily fit into one of these five divisions.

Each chapter follows a preset format. Note that no information regarding restroom facilities is given, since the balance of sites lack these amenities. Also, visitors should bring their own food and water, since these are mostly unavailable at the sites. The format used for each site contains the following information:

Habitats: Maine has a diverse number of habitats; this section gives full details on what kind of habitat or habitats you will encounter at each site.

Best time to bird: Maine's four distinct seasons, and the brief time between the key seasons, all bring with them windows of opportunity for viewing different birds. This section suggests the best times of year to visit the site.

Access: This section, when provided, notes the degree of physical activity required for birding at the site. Some sites are located in wilderness settings and require walking and hiking. Some allow for wheelchair access or have observation decks or platforms. Other sites allow visitors to do their birding from a motor vehicle. If a canoe allows greater access to a site, that is mentioned here. In no instance, however, is any type of watercraft *required* to bird the site; all sites can be birded from land.

Nearest gas, food, and lodging: This lists the nearest sources of gas, food, and lodging to each site. While many sites are in well-populated areas, many others are located in wild settings. Check this section carefully before heading out to make sure that food, fuel, and accommodations will be available if you need them.

Nearest camping: Nearby campgrounds are noted here.

For more information: Listed here are phone numbers, mailing addresses, and Web sites of managing agencies.

Directions: This section provides detailed directions that will enable you to locate the site. Also included here are map and grid references as represented in the *DeLorme: Maine Atlas and Gazetteer* (MAG). Be sure to use a current version of the MAG for the most accurate and up-to-date information. Lacking a MAG, a Maine highway map, used in conjunction with the written directions given here, will enable you to find the site.

The birds: Because an unanticipated species might be present at any given time, this section cannot be all inclusive. Also, a complete list of birds for each site would be far too lengthy to present in its entirety. What you will find here are key species, those most likely to be seen at different times of the year. Also noted here are specialty birds that may possibly be seen at this site, as well as species that are endangered, threatened, or of special interest. Finally, accidental visitors at this site are mentioned.

About this site: This section includes information regarding the physical and historical features of each site plus incidental information about the birds and the site and notes specific to the site. Pertinent land managers and organizations, any other information that may add interest, and potential hazards or dangerous conditions are noted here as well.

Nearby opportunities: This section describes nearby places for birding, as well as information of a general nature regarding nearby areas or places of interest. By combining the main site with these nearby opportunities, you can often plan a full day's birding.

Common Loon

ABA Code of Birding Ethics

FalconGuides encourage our readers to follow the American Birding Association's Code of Birding Ethics. We hope that everyone who enjoys birds and birding will always respect wildlife, its environment, and the rights of others. In any conflict of interest between birds and birders, the welfare of the birds and their environment comes first.

American Birding Association's Code of Birding Ethics

1. Promote the welfare of birds and their environment.

(a) Support the protection of important bird habitat.

(b) To avoid stressing birds or exposing them to danger, exercise restraint and caution during observation, photography, sound recording, or filming.

Limit the use of recordings and other methods of attracting birds, and never use such methods in heavily birded areas, or for attracting any species that is Threatened, Endangered, or of Special Concern, or is rare in your local area.

Keep well back from nests and nesting colonies, roosts, display areas, and important feeding sites. In such sensitive areas, if there is a need for extended observation, photography, filming, or recording, try to use a blind or hide, and take advantage of natural cover.

Use artificial light sparingly for filming or photography, especially for close-ups.

(c) Before advertising the presence of a rare bird, evaluate the potential for disturbance to the bird, its surroundings, and other people in the area, and proceed only if access can be controlled, disturbance minimized, and permission has been obtained from private landowners. The sites of rare nesting birds should be divulged only to the proper conservation authorities.

(d) Stay on roads, trails, and paths where they exist; otherwise keep habitat disturbance to a minimum.

2. Respect the law and the rights of others.

(a) Do not enter private property without the owner's explicit permission.

(b) Follow all laws, rules, and regulations governing use of roads and public areas, both at home and abroad.

(c) Practice common courtesy in contacts with other people. Your exemplary behavior will generate goodwill with birders and nonbirders alike.

3. Ensure that feeders, nest structures, and other artificial bird environments are safe.

(a) Keep dispensers, water, and food clean and free of decay or disease. It is important to feed birds continually during harsh weather.

(b) Maintain and clean nest structures regularly.

(c) If you are attracting birds to an area, ensure the birds are not exposed to predation from cats and other domestic animals, or dangers posed by artificial hazards.

4. Group birding, whether organized or impromptu, requires special care. Each individual in the group, in addition to the obligations spelled out in item nos. 1 and 2, has responsibilities as a group member.

(a) Respect the interests, rights, and skills of fellow birders, as well as people participating in other legitimate outdoor activities. Freely share your knowledge and experience, except where code 1(c) applies. Be especially helpful to beginning birders.

(b)If you witness unethical birding behavior, assess the situation, and intervene if you think it prudent. When interceding, inform the person(s) of the inappropriate action, and attempt, within reason, to have it stopped. If the behavior continues, document it, and notify appropriate individuals or organizations.

Group leader responsibilities (amateur and professional trips and tours).

(c) Be an exemplary ethical role model for the group. Teach through word and example.

(d) Keep groups to a size that limits impact on the environment and does not interfere with others using the same area.

(e) Ensure everyone in the group knows of and practices this code.

(f) Learn and inform the group of any special circumstances applicable to the areas being visited (for example, no tape recorders allowed).

(g) Acknowledge that professional tour companies bear a special responsibility to place the welfare of birds and the benefits of public knowledge ahead of the company's commercial interests. Ideally, leaders should keep track of tour sightings, document unusual occurrences, and submit records to appropriate organizations.

Please follow this code and distribute and teach it to others.

The American Birding Association's Code of Birding Ethics may be freely reproduced for distribution/dissemination. Please visit the ABA Web site at www.americanbirding.org.

White-breasted Nuthatch

Southern Maine

Southern Maine, the state's most populous region, is also the warmest. Migrating birds arrive here first. This region also has the most sandy beaches—a scarce commodity in Maine. Shorebirds and others that nest on sand dunes are more common here than in other parts of the state.

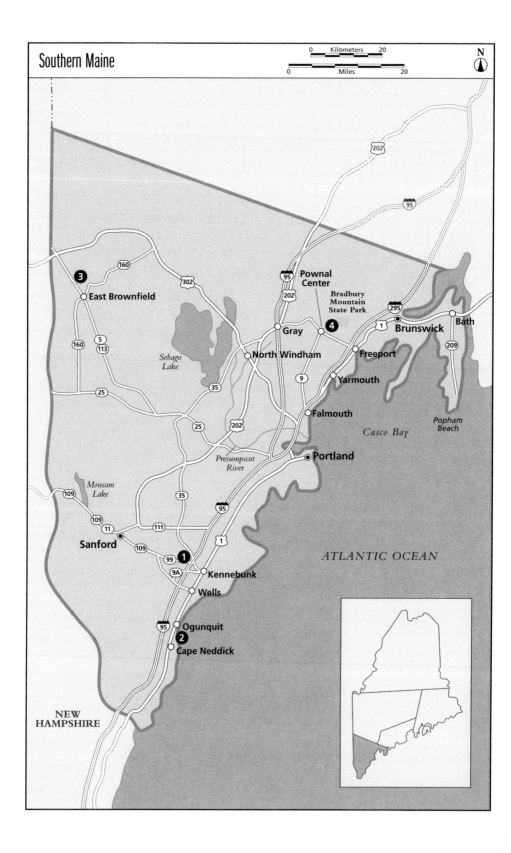

① Kennebunk Plains Wildlife Management Area

Habitats: Sandplain grasslands, pitch pine and scrub oak groups, blueberry barrens, and upland forests. Also present are a few cold spring-fed brooks and a man-made pond.

Best time to bird: Early summer through mid-summer. Barring exceedingly cold or hot weather, this means June and July.

Nearest gas, food, and lodging: Kennebunk is a vacation town and abounds with restaurants, accommodations, and places to gas up.

Nearest camping: Red Apple Campground, Sinnott Road, Kennebunkport; (207) 967-4927.

Salty Acres Campground, 277 Mills Road, Kennebunkport; (207) 967-8623.

For more information: Maine Department of Inland Fisheries and Wildlife, 284 State Street, 41 State House Station, Augusta, ME 04333-0041; (207) 287-8000; www.mefishwildlife.com.

For The Nature Conservancy, write to Maine Chapter The Nature Conservancy, 14 Main Street, Suite 401, Brunswick, ME 04011; (207) 729-5181; e-mail: naturemaine@tnc.org.

Directions: Drive north on U.S. Route 1 to Kennebunk, and look for the intersection on the left of Routes 9A and 99. Turn left (west) onto Route 99, and cross Interstate 95 on an overpass. Drive another 2 miles to a clearly signed DIF&W parking lot on the right (north) side of the road. This is the north section of the plains. To bird the south end, continue west on Route 99 for 1 mile. Make a sharp left onto McGuire Road, and drive east for 0.5 mile to another DIF&W parking lot on the right (south) side of the road. *DeLorme: Maine Atlas and Gazetteer:* Page 2, D5

The birds

Sandplain grasslands are scarce in Maine. Consequently, bird species that prefer this kind of habitat are also uncommon or rare in the state. For instance, Kennebunk Plains Wildlife Management Area (WMA) hosts one of the few colonies of Grasshopper Sparrow found in Maine. Also present are Vesper Sparrow, Upland Sandpiper, Bobolink, Eastern Meadowlark, and Horned Lark. And while certainly not uncommon, you might encounter Wild Turkey, courtesy of a program of reintroduction, by the DIF&W. Although an unmarked foot trail exists here, the best way to bird the plains is by road. Stop, get out, and scan the grasses for perching Grasshopper Sparrow. Look in the air for Upland Sandpiper and Horned Lark. And listen for birdsong of these and other species. Also spend some time watching and listening at either of the two DIF&W parking areas.

About this site

Once managed as commercial blueberry land, Kennebunk Plains WMA is jointly owned and managed by DIF&W and The Nature Conservancy. Of the 1,041 total acres of this WMA, about 600 are open grasslands. Prescribed burns are employed in order to keep the pine barrens in the early successional development stage that's so critical to the birds, plants, and other wildlife here.

Barred owls are common throughout Maine and may be seen year-round.

Of special interest at Kennebunk Plains is the northern black racer. Although this large, fast snake is common enough in other parts of the country, it is endangered in Maine. Ribbon snakes and wood turtles, two state special-concern reptiles, also occur here. A total of 14 rare plant and animal species live at Kennebunk Plains. The grasslands support the one viable stand of northern blazing star in Maine.

While all WMAs are managed for their naturally occurring wildlife, Kennebunk Plains stands out because it is home to so many different uncommon, rare, or endangered species. Please take special pains to keep your footprints invisible. We are the visitors here.

Nearby opportunities

Rachel Carson National Wildlife Refuge, in nearby Wells, has an interpretive trail with lots of birding opportunities. To get there, take US 1 in Wells and drive northeast to the intersection of Route 9. Turn right (east) onto Route 9 and drive approximately 0.9 mile to a refuge sign on the right. Turn right at this sign, and park in the parking lot.

The 1.0-mile, wheelchair-accessible gravel path is a loop, with stops at key locations and observation posts. Pine woods along the path and near the refuge headquarters hold land-based birds, and shorebirds and waterfowl are visible from the observation points. A total of 250 species of birds have been identified on or from the refuge. For more information write Refuge Manager, Rachel Carson NWR, 321 Port Road, Wells, ME 04090; or call (207) 646-9226. *DeLorme: Maine Atlas and Gazetteer:* Page 3, D1

If you have time, you might want to check out the Mousam River Wildlife Sanctuary in Kennebunk. This 38-acre parcel, part of the Kennebunk Land Trust, consists of forest and river frontage, with 2,438 feet of frontage along the Mousam River. For more information write Kennebunk Land Trust, 11 York Street, Kennebunk, ME 04043; call (207) 985-8734; or e-mail kennbklt@gwi.net.

② Marginal Way

Habitats: Atlantic Ocean.

Best time to bird: November through April.

Nearest gas, food, and lodging: Ogunquit abounds in restaurants, shops, accommodations, and gas stations.

Nearest camping: Cape Neddick Oceanside Campground, Cape Neddick; (207) 363-4366. Libby's Oceanside Camp, York Harbor; (207) 363-4171.

For more information: Town of Ogunquit; (207) 646-5139. Cliff House Resort and Spa, Shore Road, P.O. Box 2274, Ogunquit, ME 03907; (207) 361-1000; info@cliffhouse maine.com. For more information about Ogunquit and Marginal Way, see *Maine Off the Beaten Path* (The Globe Pequot Press, 2006) and *Hiking Maine* (The Globe Pequot Press, 2002).

Directions: In Cape Neddick, head north on U.S. Route 1A to Pine Hill Road, on the right (east) side of US 1A. Follow Pine Hill Road north to where it joins Shore Road in Perkins Cove in Ogunquit. Parking areas are located off Shore Road and on Cottage Street, in Perkins Cove. On Shore Road follow signage for the path at Marginal Way. *DeLorme: Maine Atlas and Gazetteer:* Page 1, A5

The birds

This is a prime site for a variety of seabirds, especially those that spend winters off the Maine coast. Common species include cormorants, Long-tailed Duck, and Common Eider. Occasionally King Eider show up here. Other ducks include American Black Duck, Bufflehead, Gadwall, Common Goldeneye, and White-winged Scoter.

Marginal Way is famous for its population of Harlequin Duck. The Maine Department of Inland Fisheries and Wildlife (DIF&W) listed Harlequin Duck as threatened in 1997. As of 2006 DIF&W estimated the eastern North American population of harlequins at somewhere between 1,800 and 2,000 individuals. Of these, about 1,300 spend the winter in Maine. Harlequins are seldom seen because they spend much of their time on the barren shores of Maine's offshore islands. However, several flocks spend the winter off Ogunquit, and these are what visitors to Marginal Way see. A visit here is by far the easiest way to see Harlequin Duck.

Also present are Common and Red-throated Loon, Ring-billed Gull, Black Guillemot, Herring Gull, Great Black-backed Gull, American Crow, and Fish Crow.

Sometimes winter storms will carry oceangoing birds that do not normally visit the coast in to shore near Marginal Way. Such rare occurrences cannot be predicted. However, the chance to see one of these unexpected visitors adds a bit of drama and flavor to a visit here.

The wild roses and cedar trees along the way harbor other birds. Expect to see or hear American Robin, Black-capped Chickadee, common crows, House Sparrow,

Herring Gull and other seabirds are a common sight along Marginal Way.

Mourning Dove, Northern Cardinal, Northern Mockingbird, and Rock Pigeon. Beginning in March and continuing through October, Turkey Vulture occasionally soars above the path.

About this site

The best birding occurs in the off-season for tourists. In summer Marginal Way is a haven for walkers, artists, photographers, and anyone else who likes expansive ocean views. In fact, about two million people visit Marginal Way each year. In fall, winter, and early spring, though, casual visitors are fewer, and many visitors at that time are birders. Another point in favor of a visit to Marginal Way is the 1.25-mile wheelchair-accessible path.

While summer visitors delight in scrambling down to the water's edge, this can be extremely dangerous in winter. Slippery when wet, the rocky ledges here are even more slippery when coated with a layer of ice. Benches situated at regular intervals along the path allow for comfort while scanning the water. Dress warmly; if you plan to sit on a bench, it's a good idea to carry a pad, small pillow, or even one of the "hot seats" used by hunters to place between you and the cold surface.

Be sure to bring extra clothes to put on if you need them. Even in fall and early spring, a damp day combined with a sea breeze can make you feel miserable if you are not properly dressed.

The Town of Ogunquit owns Marginal Way. Admission is free.

Nearby opportunities

On the coast, a little more than 3 miles south of Marginal Way, Cliff House Resort and Spa sits upon Bald Head, a favorite sport for wintertime birding. Ogunquit is a tourist town, full of art galleries, souvenir shops, resorts, and restaurants of all descriptions.

③ Brownfield Bog Wildlife Management Area

Habitats: Open-water wetlands, seasonally flooded wetlands, shrub wetlands; emergent marshes, bogs; old fields; mature upland forest; open water with aquatic-bed vegetation.

Best time to bird: Visit here any time spring through fall, roughly May through October, and you will encounter a great variety of bird species. As with so many other water-based WMAs, June is a time of hectic bird activity.

Access: Significant birding can be done by walking the wood roads and also from the parking area. Except during times of severe drought, it is advisable to bring water-resistant boots, since the roads can be wet and/or muddy. Birders can also launch a canoe near the parking lot to explore the vastness of the bog.

Nearest food and lodging: Look for restaurants, inns, and bed-and-breakfast establishments in nearby Fryeburg.

Nearest camping: Shannon's Saco River Sanctuary, Brownfield; (207) 452-2774; www.shannonscamping.com. Woodland Acres Camp 'N' Canoe, Brownfield; (207) 935-2529; www.woodlandacres.com.

For more information: Contact Maine Department of Inland Fisheries and Wildlife in Augusta at (207) 287-8000, or call Region A Headquarters in Gray at (207) 657-2345.

Directions: In East Brownfield, look for the intersection of Routes 5/113 and Route 160. From here drive about 2 miles east on Route 160 to the intersection with Lord Hill Road on the left (west) side of road. At this intersection you'll see a dirt road on the left and a sign for Brownfield Bog WMA. Drive to the end of the dirt road (slightly less than 1 mile) to the parking area and boat launch site. *DeLorme: Maine Atlas and Gazetteer:* Page 4, B2

The birds

Maine Department of Inland Fisheries and Wildlife (DIF&W) specifically manages Brownfield Bog Wildlife Management Area (WMA) for waterfowl, and one hundred nesting boxes have been erected to facilitate nesting.

Duck species to be found here include Mallard, Hooded Merganser, Ring-necked Duck, Wood Duck, Common Goldeneye, American Black Duck, and Green-winged and Blue-winged Teal. Also here are Canada Goose, Belted Kingfisher, Great Blue Heron, Pied-billed Grebe, Marsh Wren, American Bittern, Osprey, Virginia Rail, and Northern Waterthrush. Willow Flycatcher, Blue-gray Gnatcatcher, and Yellow-throated Vireo breed at Brownfield Bog WMA. A variety of hawks, upland game birds, warblers, and a variety of forest birds are also present. A rarity, Sedge Wren, is noted here. In general, marshbird diversity is exceptional, and waterfowl numbers are excellent.

The spring warbler migration draws a large number of different warblers, including but not limited to Pine, Palm, Black-and-white, and Yellow-rumped Warbler. The total list of bird species for Brownfield Bog WMA is staggering, and the outline given here only scratches the surface.

Wild turkeys are a common roadside sight year-round.

About this site

This 5,700-acre WMA stands out as a significant wild area. While the nearby Saco River teems with canoe and kayak traffic in summer, Brownfield Bog WMA sees relatively little pressure. DIF&W maintains an access road and parking area at the bog. To illustrate just how great birding is here, the Brownfield Bog WMA parking area was selected as a "Big Sit" site in October 2007. The Big Sit is a continuous 24-hour bird count done within the confines of a 17-foot diameter circle.

While ample birding exists around the parking area, lots of opportunity exists for walking around the WMA on unimproved roads. In addition to managing for waterfowl, DIF&W also manages the WMA for upland birds and animals. Specially controlled timber harvests result in improved habitat for Ruffed Grouse and American Woodcock. Old, dying trees are left as nest trees, and oak trees are left as is in order to provide mast. As with many other WMAs noted in this book, a canoe opens up a whole new world of birding. Put your canoe in near the small DIF&W building by the parking area.

The bog hosts some interesting plants, including northern pitcher, sundew, and rhodora. Open-water areas are laced with aquatic-bed vegetation. Wild plant fanciers will have a banner day when visiting here for the first time.

Nearby opportunities

For anyone spending time in Southern Maine, a visit to the Maine Wildlife Park operated by DIF&W is a must-do. This 200-acre park features wild birds and animals (many are here for rehabilitation and are slated for eventual release back into the wild), programs for adults and youngsters, interactive exhibits, interpretive trails, and much more. Besides the hawks, owls, and Bald Eagle usually on exhibit here, free-roaming birds seen by visitors include Pileated Woodpecker, various hawks, Wood Duck, Wild Turkey, Bald Eagle, and Bohemian Waxwing. Wildlife photographers know the Wildlife Park as a prime location to get close-up shots of a wide variety of birds and animals.

The park is open 9:30 a.m. to 4:30 p.m. daily from mid–April to November 11. To reach the park from the intersection of U.S. Route 302 and Route 115 in North Windham, drive east on Route 115 to Gray, turn left onto Route 26, and drive for 3.4 miles to the Maine Wildlife Park on the right. A large sign marks the entrance.

For more information write Maine Wildlife Park, 56 Game Farm Road, Gray, ME 04039; call (207) 657-4977, ext. 0; or e-mail mainewildlifepark@mainerr.com. *DeLorme: Maine Atlas and Gazetteer:* Page 5, B3

4 Bradbury Mountain State Park

Habitats: Open mountain summit, granite ledge.

Best time to bird: The spring hawk migration is highly recommended; it begins in mid-April and lasts through early May. The fall migration begins in mid-September and continues through early October. In summer visitors here can still hope to see soaring Turkey Vulture and perhaps a passing eagle. Land-based songbirds are active early mornings and evenings in summer.

Nearest gas, food, and lodging: Freeport has many great restaurants and plenty of places to stay and fill your tank.

Nearest camping: Camping is available at Wolfe's Neck Woods State Park (207-865-4465 summer; 207-624-6075 winter) and at Thomas Point Beach and Campground in Brunswick (877-872-4321).

For more information: Maine Bureau of Parks and Lands, 22 State House Station, Augusta, ME 04333; call (207) 688-4712. Also see chapters on Bradbury Mountain and Wolfe's Neck Woods State Parks in *Hiking Maine* (The Globe Pequot Press, 2002).

Directions: In Falmouth take Route 9 north to Pownal Center. Drive through the center and look for a sign on the right (east) side of road for Bradbury Mountain State Park. If you go past the sign, you will see a huge, round cattle pound on the left. This historic artifact is made of laid-up fieldstone. *DeLorme: Maine Atlas and Gazetteer:* Page 5, C5

The birds

Bradbury Mountain is a prime southern Maine location for watching migrating birds of prey. Spend a day here in spring and you can see 100 or more Broad-winged Hawk. Also look for Red-tailed Hawk, Sharp-shinned Hawk, and kestrels. If you are lucky you might even spy a Peregrine Falcon. You will probably see Turkey Vulture and possibly Bald Eagle and Osprey. For the maximum number of migrating birds, best viewing happens when the wind blows from the southwest.

The rest of the park, including the bulk of the mountain with the exception of the summit, is forested with mixed-growth hardwoods and softwoods. In spring, especially May, look here for woodland warblers.

If possible, plan to spend a day atop the mountain. Be sure to bring a camera, binoculars, and a spotting scope if you have one.

About this site

Bradbury Mountain is an off-the-beaten-path state park that offers hiking, camping, and of course birding. The mountain summit, the highest point for many miles around, offers superb views of Casco Bay, parts of Sebago Lake, and on a clear day, Mount Washington in nearby New Hampshire.

Osprey are a favorite of birders at Bradbury Mountain State Park.

Nearby opportunities

Wolfe's Neck State Park, in Freeport, is situated on the end of a long, narrow peninsula bordered to the west by the Harraseeket River and to the east by Casco Bay. Hiking trails lead through forests, with good views of the Harraseeket River and the estuarine areas of Little River. Casco Bay Trail follows the shoreline of the bay. Look for rafts of waterfowl just offshore, plus Great Blue Heron wading along the shore. Woodland areas offer chances to observe migrating warblers in spring, as well as thrushes and flycatchers. Osprey nesting on nearby Googins Island can be observed from the mainland.

Wolfe's Neck also offers a 0.5-mile barrier-free trail, guided nature tours, and ongoing nature programs. For more information write to Maine Bureau of Parks and Lands, 22 State House Station, Augusta, ME 04333; or call (207) 865-4465 April through October or (207) 624-6080 November through March. *DeLorme: Maine Atlas and Gazetteer:* Page 6, D1

Midcoast Maine

Midcoast Maine, a place of rural roads winding down long peninsulas, also boasts rolling hills, lakes and streams, and small villages. Dairy farmers manage to eke out a living despite pressures from developers to sell. The Midcoast Region contains a number of state parks and wildlife management areas, all prime birding sites. Islands off the Midcoast Region host rare and fascinating seabirds, and commercial boat operators here take visitors for birding cruises on the Atlantic Ocean.

Midcoast Maine

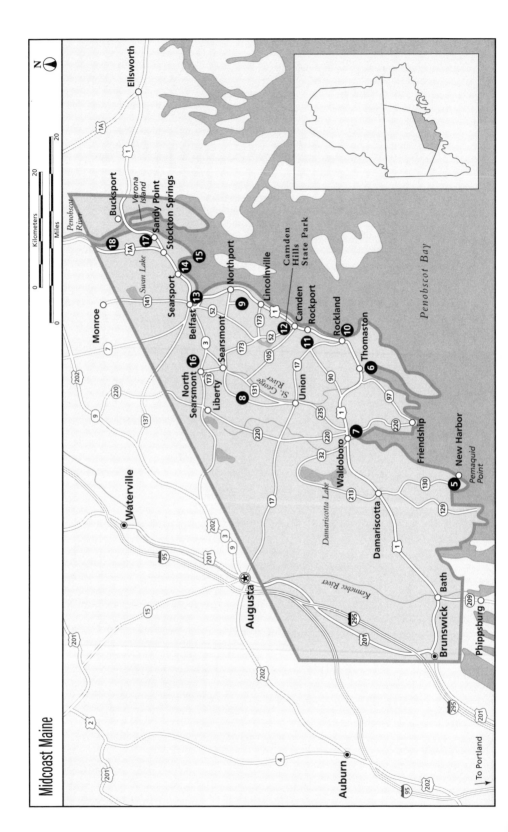

⑤ Pemaquid Point

Habitats: Rocky point at the end of a peninsula that projects out into the Gulf of Maine.

Best time to bird: You will see plenty of birds here year-round. However, if you arrive in November or December after a fall storm, you may have an opportunity to view a rarity that was blown in by the storm.

Nearest gas, food, and lodging: All can be found in nearby New Harbor.

Nearest camping: Sherwood Forest Campground, Pemaquid; (800) 274-1593.

For more information: See *Maine Off the Beaten Path* (The Globe Pequot Press, 2006).

Directions: From U.S. Route 1 in Damariscotta, drive south on Routes 129 and 130. Where these two roads fork a few miles down the road, bear left (southeast) on Route 130 (Bristol Road). Continue following Route 130 to its end at Pemaquid Point. Total distance from Damariscotta is about 12 miles. *DeLorme: Maine Atlas and Gazetteer:* Page 7, C3

The birds

A great variety of seabirds show up at Pemaquid Point. Razorbill, Bonaparte's Gull, Black-legged Kittiwake, Black Guillemot, Red-necked Grebe, Common Loon, Red-throated Loon, and Northern Gannet are all regular visitors. Sea ducks abound, and these sometimes include King Eider and Harlequin Duck. Atlantic Puffin is possible, but don't expect them. Purple Sandpiper is seen along the point, and you may see Glaucous Gull and Iceland Gull. These are only a smattering of the smorgasbord of seabirds at Pemaquid Point. If you are new to birding, be sure to carry a good field guide—you will need it here. If you are visiting from another state, be sure to bring a camera; you may well encounter a bird for your life list. Note that while Bonaparte's Gull, Black-legged Kittiwake, and Razorbill are common in winter, you really need a spotting scope to see them. Look out to sea, and scan the water carefully. Some birders consider Pemaquid Point one of the best sites on the Maine coast to see Razorbill.

About this site

Visiting Pemaquid Point is like going out to sea, but without a boat. The peninsula is long and relatively narrow, extending well out in the ocean, which explains why it is such a great place for seabirds. For history-minded individuals, it's also like going back in time. David Ingram, who walked from the Gulf of Mexico to Nova Scotia in 1569 after being set ashore by Captain John Hawkins, is said to have tarried at Pemaquid Point. And in 1632 the famed pirate Dixie Bull sailed into Pemaquid and sacked the place. Today, Fisherman's Museum occupies the lighthouse at Pemaquid Point.

Long a favorite destination for artists and photographers, Pemaquid Point offers shore-bound birders a rare chance to see a great variety of seabirds.

Nearby opportunities

The 60-foot *Hardy III* sails out of New Harbor in summer on special birding cruises. Hardy's offers several different options, including puffin cruises. For more information call (800) 278-3346.

Limited parking is available along Route 32, about 0.1 mile north of New Harbor. This is a popular local spot, and in summer, chances of getting off the road are slight. But in winter you may find this spot unoccupied. It's a better bet, though, to park in New Harbor and walk north along Route 32. This affords several excellent viewing opportunities along the protected harbor. Flocks of Common Eider and large groups of Mallard are regulars here.

⑥ R. Waldo Tyler Wildlife Management Area— Weskeag Marsh

Habitats: Tidal salt marsh, some upland fields and forests.

Best time to bird: Birding is good year-round, but summer is the very best time. From approximately Memorial Day (the unofficial beginning of summer in Maine) through September, nesting birds, waterfowl, and shorebirds are in evidence. Look for Least Sandpiper, too.

Migrating waterfowl and shorebirds show up here in early spring, as soon as the snow melts, which in this area is mid- or late March. It is then that Common Snipe return, and American Woodcock search for ground that is free of snow. Other shorebirds seen in spring include Semipalmated and Least Sandpiper, Greater and Lesser Yellowlegs, Dunlin, and Ruddy Turnstone, to name a few.

The fall migration brings many more shorebirds and waterfowl. Also be on the alert for Northern Harrier in fall.

Winter brings owls. Snowy and Short-eared Owl, a special treat, have been noted.

Rough-legged Hawk are possible as well. Snow Bunting form flocks now, and Lapland Longspur and Horned Lark may accompany them.

Again, the birds listed here are but a tiny fraction of what you can find at R. Waldo Tyler WMA.

Nearest gas, food, and lodging: Thomaston has plenty of fine restaurants, and motels dot U.S. Route 1 in Rockland. Gas is readily available along US 1.

Nearest camping: Camden Hills State Park, Camden; (207) 236-3109 from May 1 through October 15 and (207) 236-0849 from October 16 through April 30. Megunticook Campground by the sea, Rockport; (207) 594-2428.

For more information: Maine Department of Inland Fisheries and Wildlife, 284 State Street, 41 State House Station, Augusta, ME 04333-0041; (207) 287-8000; www.mefish wildlife.com.

Directions: From Thomaston drive south on U.S. Route 1. Just outside of town, look for the large stack of the Dragon Cement Plant and for Buttermilk Lake, a secondary road on your left, just past the plant. Turn onto Buttermilk Lane and drive about 1 mile. Look for a culvert by the marsh and a small roadside turnout on the right (west) side of the road. Just past this, and on the same side of the road on top of a hill, is another small turnout. This site gives you a bird's-eye view of the marsh. However, the turnout by the culvert affords a better opportunity to walk out into the marsh, as well as scan the marsh from the roadside. *DeLorme: Maine Atlas and Gazetteer:* Page 8, A3

The birds

This WMA is the northernmost nesting site for Saltmarsh Sharp-tailed Sparrow. R. Waldo Tyler WMA is a haven for shorebirds, waterfowl, grassland birds, and wading birds of all sorts, many more than can be listed here. A variety of hawks and owls are seen here too, as are several different gulls, along with Osprey and Bald

Tidal Weskeag Marsh is the northernmost nesting site for the Saltmarsh Sharp-tailed Sparrow.

Eagle. In short, this ranks among the best sites in Maine for spotting vast numbers of interesting species of birds. To add even more spice to this already fabulous site, three rarities have been sighted here in the past 10 years: Garganey, Eurasian Wigeon, and Ruff.

About this site

Like all the other state WMAs, this is owned and administered by the Maine Department of Inland Fisheries and Wildlife. And, like the other WMAs listed in this book, the R. Waldo Tyler WMA is totally undeveloped.

Birding can be done from one of the roadside turnoffs; you can also walk out in the marsh. This suggestion is accompanied by a caveat. The marsh contains ditches and channels, often hidden by marsh grass; stepping in one of these unawares can cause a sprained ankle, or worse. I recommend knee-length, water-proof boots and a walking stick. When walking where you can't see the ground very well, use the stick to part the grass in front of you. With caution, you can get around a large part of the marsh on foot. In spring, summer, and into fall, be sure to bring lots of insect repellent to keep the mosquitoes at bay.

You will want binoculars if you walk out in the marsh. A scope will serve you well for scanning from the roadside. There are no facilities of any kind here, so be sure and bring food and drink.

Nearby opportunities

Farther down the Weskeag River (R. Waldo Tyler WMA is adjacent to the Weskeag River), The Midcoast Chapter of the National Audubon Society maintains the three-acre Weskeag River Preserve. The parcel contains conifer growth as well as 300 feet of shore frontage on the Weskeag River. Shorebirds and land-based birds of conifer forests are found here. To reach Weskeag River Preserve, drive south on Buttermilk Lane (the same road that R. Waldo Tyler WMA is on . . . just continue past the WMA) and turn right (south) at the intersection with Route 73. Stay on Route 73 for a little over 2 miles, and turn left (east) onto Waterman Beach Road. Weskeag River Preserve is 0.1 mile down Waterman Beach Road, on the left. The preserve is not indicated on the *Maine Atlas and Gazetteer,* but if it were, it would be on Page 8, A3, about 1 inch below R. Waldo Tyler WMA. Call Midcoast Audubon at (207) 832-2001.

⑦ Guy VanDuyn Refuge

Habitats: Upland forest comprising mature white pine, spruce, and red oak; grassy fields with honeysuckle shrubs around the edges; islands in the middle of the river; tidal salt marsh.

Best time to bird: From May through August, morning and evening birding is excellent for songbirds in upland sections, particularly around the edge of the field. Early morning should be the absolute best time here. Late August and September should see an influx of shorebirds, including Common Snipe. October and November are good for ducks at high tide.

Access: The John Steenis Trail provides foot access. This may be slippery in wet weather. A fairly steep incline makes for moderately strenuous walking. At low tide, much of the

tidal marsh is accessible by foot. However, as with all tidal marshes, caution is called for because of narrow but deep rivulets carved into the clay over the centuries. Grasses sometimes obscure these, so you need to watch your feet at all times.

Nearest food and lodging: Waldoboro has both food and lodging, including bed-and-breakfast establishments.

Nearest camping: Duck Puddle Campground, Nobleboro; (207) 563-5608. Town Line Campsites, Nobleboro; (207) 832-7055.

For more information: For both Guy VanDuyn Refuge and Nelson Nature Preserve, contact Mid-Coast Audubon Society, P.O. Box 862, Rockland, ME 04841-0862, (207) 832-2001; www.midcoastaudubon.org.

Directions: Beginning in downtown Waldoboro, drive south on Route 220 for 1.5 miles. On the right, see a gravel turnoff and a small sign for Guy VanDuyn Refuge. Park here; this is the trailhead for the John Steenis Trail. *DeLorme: Maine Atlas and Gazetteer:* Page 7, A5

The birds

Birds likely to be found here include woodland songbirds; warblers in the upland section; and waterfowl and shorebirds, including ducks and geese, on the river and marsh. Bald Eagle and Osprey are always a possibility, especially around the marsh and river. In late summer look for Common Snipe; Virginia Rail are possible in the short grass of the marsh. Canada Goose are always a possibility. Many geese now remain in Maine year-round rather than migrating.

About this site

Owned and managed by the Mid-Coast Audubon Society, this 30-acre parcel is open to the public year-round. Except for the trails and a few birdhouses placed on trees here and there, the site has little or no evidence of human intervention.

The John Steenis Trail begins along the road by a wooden trail sign that is partially obscured by ferns and weeds in summer. No other sign or indications of a refuge exist. The trip from Route 220 to the tidal flats is mostly downhill, and beginning at about the halfway point (the trail is about 0.6 mile long), the incline becomes fairly steep. Only persons in good physical condition should venture here.

A number of cavity-nesting birds are attracted to these nesting boxes.

This is not to say that the trail is particularly strenuous, but it certainly requires a bit of effort, especially the walk back.

This site is typical of many of Maine's little-known and mostly unadvertised places. Although small, it has a diverse geography and offers much in the way of birding. Rarely will you see more than one or two vehicles here, and most of the time you can have the entire refuge to yourself. The managing agency requests that you stay on trails, but that is hardly a hindrance to the dedicated birder. An exception to this is the field about halfway down the hill. The trail, such as it is, ends here and begins on the other side. Birders may secure themselves along the edge of the field for a front-row seat for over 80 different species of songbirds. Binoculars are a definite plus for the wooded areas and the field. A scope, however, is preferred for scanning the tidal marsh and far-off Medomak River.

Nearby opportunities

Nelson Nature Preserve in nearby Friendship sees mostly local birders. The casual visitor could pass by and not realize the place exists, since it is off the beaten path and not signed. Nelson Preserve comprises 95 acres, with narrow trails leading through dense spruce woods. Moss covers rocks, stumps, and dead trees, prompting a feeling of quiet and serenity. Trails, marked with metal triangles, wind through the preserve.

Goose River bounds part of the preserve, and the riparian habitat provides excellent spring warbler habitat. The upland sections here host birds of the thick forest. Look for woodpeckers, thrushes, Black-capped Chickadee and other forest birds. Combined with a visit to Guy VanDuyn Refuge, a trip here can easily fill an entire day.

To reach Nelson Nature Preserve from Guy VanDuyn Refuge, drive south on Route 220 (Friendship Road) to the town of Friendship. Here, at a stop sign, Route 220 becomes Route 97. Drive left (east) on Route 97 into town. At 1.3 miles from downtown Friendship, look on the right for a brown barn that sells antiques. This is at the start of a sharp curve. Just past the antiques shop, at a bend on the corner, look for a drive on the left. The lower section of the drive is paved. Turn onto this slightly uphill drive to a small parking area lined with northern bay bushes and rugosa rose. Here a small map indicates the various trails. *DeLorme: Maine Atlas and Gazetteer:* Page 8, B1

⑧ Appleton Ridge

Habitats: Open fields, cultivated blueberry land, Christmas tree farmland.

Best time to bird: Various species possible year-round. American Woodcock arrive as early as March, depending on how soon snow cover dissipates. Summer and fall are best for grassland birds, especially June, July, and August. Beginning in late August and lasting through September, the fall hawk migration can provide exciting birding.

Access: The entire area covered in this chapter is easily accessed by automobile. However, in winter part of the road may not be adequately maintained; caution is advised from December through March.

Nearest food and lodging: Camden and Rockport are quintessential tourist towns containing all amenities.

Nearest camping: Megunticook Campground by the Sea, Rockport; (207) 594-2428 or (800) 884-2428. Camden Hills State Park, Camden; (207) 236-3109 or (207) 236-0849 (off-season).

For more information: Appleton Ridge is a geographic location, not an organized governmental entity. There is no managing agency.

Directions: From the intersection of U.S. Route 1 and Route 3 in Belfast, drive west on Route 3 for about 12 miles to North Searsmont. Look for a sign and a gravel parking lot by a pond and wetland on the right (north) side of the road. This is the James Dorso Wildlife Management Area (see site 16). Continue past this point for about 100 feet, and look for New England Road on the left. This is marked by a road sign, but the post sits in the ditch and consequently the sign is not up to standard height. Take New England Road for 3.5 miles to the intersection with Routes 173 and 131. Turn right (west) and go about 0.2 mile to where Route 131 branches to the left (south). Follow Route 131 south 0.6 mile to Ridge Road on the right. Follow Ridge Road for 8.2 miles to where it intersects Route 131. Return by the route you came, or turn left onto Route 131 to return to Searsmont. *DeLorme: Maine Atlas and Gazetteer:* Page 14, C1 and C2

The birds

Migrating hawks, especially Broad-winged and Sharp-shinned, are key here. Summertime favorites include Meadowlark, Savannah Sparrow, Bobolink, Upland Sandpiper, and Horned Lark. Migrating American Pipit and Short-eared Owl are possible.

On still spring evenings you can hear the nasal sound of American Woodcock taking part in their courtship rituals. The ridge also attracts woodcocks in late September and October, as birds from regions far to the north set down in the scrub and pioneer growth alongside many of the large fields.

In winter, Snow Bunting are possible. If you stop anywhere along the ridge on a still winter's night, you may hear Barred and Great Horned Owl.

About this site

Appleton Ridge is a geographic wonder—an 8-mile-long backbone of open land with far-reaching vistas on both sides, a scaled-down version of Skyline Drive.

Chokecherries and sumac along the road and at Appleton Ridge provide food and protection for birds.

Once considered among the loveliest sites in Maine, development has partially despoiled this natural treasure. Until recently, open fields with accompanying hedgerows, alder thickets, and boulder-strewn blueberry land invited local people to come, sit, and enjoy nature. In many instances, such idyllic settings have been converted to house lots. Despite this, much of the ridge remains development-free.

Appleton Ridge runs approximately northeast to southwest, encompassing portions of the towns of Searsmont, Appleton, and Union. Its unique position stands as a beacon to migrating birds. However, you must remember that this is private land; trespassing is, for the most part, forbidden. You may, however, park alongside the road and scan the fields and barren land at many points along the drive. Several turnouts exist where people do just that, although such turnouts are often nothing more than ledge outcroppings alongside the road.

For the most part, you will want a set of binoculars. A scope is ideal for this site, since you have visual access to such a far-reaching, wide-open area.

There are no amenities available at this site. You must bring your own food and water. Always bring extra clothing, especially in spring and fall. Evening birding at these times can be a chilly proposition, and a sweater or sweatshirt will be welcome.

You can select your own spots along the ridge. As a roadside birding site, opportunities are many and varied and change with the seasons. To make the most of your trip here, begin on one end of the ridge and work your way to the other.

Nearby opportunities

Merryspring, a 66-acre park and education center, features plantings of various wild and cultivated flowers, herbs, and shrubs. The park's nature trails are open to the public daily, free of charge, and the park offers workshops on a variety of nature topics.

The flower plantings make Merryspring a special place for Ruby-throated Hummingbird. A visit here early on a summer morning is practically guaranteed to result in close-up hummingbird sightings and a great opportunity for hummingbird photos. To reach Merryspring, drive east on US 1 in Rockport to the intersection of US 1 and Route 90. Continue east on US 1 for 1 mile, and look for Conway Road on the left just beyond the shopping plaza. Drive 0.3 mile to the end of Conway Road, and look for a sign for Merryspring. For more information contact Merryspring, P.O. Box 893, Camden, ME 04843; (207) 236-2239; e-mail mersprng@gwi.net.

⑨ Knight Pond

Habitats: Knight Pond Road, a mostly unpaved rural country lane, leads through reverting farmland as well as mature oak forests. Wyman Park, at the beach at Knight Pond, provides access to the pond and also to surrounding wetlands.

Best time to bird: Migrating warblers visit the brushy area around the pond beginning in mid-May. June brings breeding waterbirds. In October migrating American Woodcock land in alder covers near the pond. Also in October and November, mornings and evenings are good times to see ducks and Canada Goose as they drop in during their fall migration.

Access: Access is as easy as slowly driving down the road with your window open. At Wyman Park you can easily walk about the shore of Knight Pond. A gravel launch site makes it easy to launch a canoe.

Nearest food and lodging: Northport has several restaurants and motels along U.S. Route 1.

Nearest camping: Northport Travel Park Campground, Northport; (207) 338-2077. Camden Hills State Park, Camden; (207) 236-3091 (May 1 through October 15) or (207) 236-0849 (October 16 through April 30).

For more information: Call the Northport Town Office at (207) 338-3819, or e-mail northport@gwi.net.

Directions: From US 1 in Northport, turn left (west) onto Beech Hill Road; drive for 2.4 miles to the intersection with Knights Pond Road. Turn left (south) onto Knights Pond Road, and follow this road for 0.5 mile to where the pavement ends and gravel begins. From here it's another 2.4 miles to Wyman Park on Knight Pond. *DeLorme: Maine Atlas and Gazetteer:* Page 14, C4 and C5

The birds

Beginning on the Knight Pond Road, look for Cedar Waxwing feeding on wild berries. This is a good spot to see migrating spring warblers. As the road makes the transition from reverting farmland to mature forest, look and listen for Northern Cardinal. Pileated and other woodpeckers are seen here, as are Ruffed Grouse and American Woodcock. Knight Pond is a breeding site for Canada Goose, Common Loon, and a number of ducks. Osprey glide over the pond, seeking bass and pickerel.

About this site

As with so many other excellent birding sites described in this book, Knight Pond is well known to a handful of local birders and virtually unknown to others. It is worth taking your time as you drive down the nearly 2-mile-long dirt road leading to the pond. Various points along the oak-lined road allow for vehicles to pull off and park. You might want to come here early in the morning, leave your vehicle, and walk up and down the road with a set of binoculars. If you do this late in afternoon, you may well see a Ruffed Grouse or two along the road, picking up gravel for their crop. Listen closely and you might also hear a Northern Cardinal and any of several varieties of woodpeckers.

Town Landing at Bayside is a good place to scan for seabirds.

The pond itself may be birded from Wyman Park. Loons, ducks, and geese are usually present during times of open water. But a canoe really allows you to explore this shallow, weedy pond to the fullest. In addition to the birdlife, the scenery here is spectacular, especially when viewed from the water. Hills and mountains—with Ducktrap Mountain, to the immediate south of the pond, a prominent feature—ring Knight Pond.

Another benefit of a birding trip here via canoe is that since 102-acre Knight Pond is so shallow (only 13 feet maximum depth), motorboats don't venture here. In the unlikely event that you encounter other boats here, they will probably be other hand-propelled craft.

Knight Pond and nearby environs are good for at least a half-day's adventure. And if you like fishing (Knight Pond contains smallmouth and largemouth bass, pickerel, and yellow perch), you could easily make a full day of it.

Wyman Park is owned by the town of Northport and has plenty of parking spaces available. In summer you may find people swimming or picnicking here.

Nearby opportunities

Nearby, the incorporated village of Bayside offers a comfortable platform from which to view gulls and other seabirds on Penobscot Bay. The town wharf extends out into the bay, and if you bring a cushion, you will have a comfortable seat on one of the wooden benches. Binoculars will help you to scan the bay for gulls, terns, and other seabirds. This facility is open year-round. In summer you will find people fishing and swimming. Fall, winter, and early spring are probably better times to look for interesting seabirds. If you come in winter, you may well encounter Barrow's Goldeneye, which are often seen a short distance up the coast in Belfast. *DeLorme: Maine Atlas and Gazetteer:* Page 14, B5

⑩ Breakwater Park

Habitats: Granite block structure projecting nearly 1 mile into Penobscot Bay, separating Rockland Harbor from the bay. A limited amount of gravel-beach shoreline.

Best time to bird: Year-round, but November through April present the best opportunities to see key birds.

Access: A slight downhill walk to the breakwater from the parking lot is easily accomplished. However, the breakwater itself can be tricky walking because of gaps between the granite blocks and the general unevenness of the surface. Winter can see freezing spray, especially when high tide is accompanied by strong winds.

Nearest gas, food, and lodging: Rockland has numerous restaurants and hotels. Glen Cove has motels and cottages. Gas is available along U.S. Route 1.

Nearest camping: Camden Hills State Park, Camden; (207) 236-3109 from May 1 through October 15 and (207) 236-0849 from October 16 through April 30. Megunticook Campground by the Sea, Rockport; (207) 594-2428.

For more information: City of Rockland, 270 Pleasant Street, Rockland, ME 04841; (207) 594-8431; e-mail info@ci.rockland.me.us.

For information about the lighthouse, contact Friends of the Rockland Breakwater Lighthouse, P.O. Box 741, Rockland, ME 04841; (207) 785-4609; e-mail brkwater@midcoast.com.

Directions: From US 1 drive north through Rockland; look for Waldo Avenue on the right, just past Littlefield Baptist Church. Turn right (east) onto Waldo Avenue and proceed 0.5 mile to a sign for Shore Road on the right, just before the entrance to Samoset Resort. Follow this road a short distance to the end at the Rockland Breakwater Park parking lot. *DeLorme: Maine Atlas and Gazetteer:* Page 14, E4

The birds

Of key interest here are Purple Sandpiper, winter visitors from the Arctic. Look for these foraging among the huge granite blocks that form the breakwater, picking around seaweed for small marine creatures. Purple Sandpiper remain here at least until April. Common and King Eider may be visible from the breakwater in winter. Watch also for Great Cormorant. Bohemian Waxwing may be seen searching for whatever natural fruit and berries they find clinging to trees and shrubs. Look for these in winter along the edge of the Samoset Resort Golf Course, which abuts Breakwater Park. In fall look for American Golden Plover on the golf course.

In summer the customary retinue of seabirds can be seen from the breakwater. Look for Herring Gull, Double-crested Cormorant, Common Tern, and Common Loon. Laughing Gull are possible, as are Bald Eagle and Osprey.

About this site

Needing protection for their harbor, in the 1880s the City of Rockland built Rockland Breakwater. The brick-and-wood Rockland Breakwater Lighthouse, at

This 1-mile granite breakwater brings the birder to the birds. Beside ducks and a variety of gulls, Rockland Breakwater hosts Purple Sandpiper, winter visitors from the Arctic regions.

the very end of the breakwater, was built in 1888; the light station was officially established in 1902.

The breakwater allows those who want to see ocean birds to do so without benefit of a boat. Views from the ocean (east) side extend to, and past, the island of Vinalhaven. Lobster fishermen set their traps close to the breakwater, providing visitors with a close-up view of lobster-harvesting activities. The breakwater is a popular fishing site.

The Breakwater Lighthouse is owned by the City of Rockland and leased to Friends of the Rockland Breakwater Lighthouse. *DeLorme: Maine Atlas and Gazetteer:* Page 14, E4

Nearby opportunities

Rockland Harbor hosts a large number of gulls, ducks, and other waterbirds. The harbor is visible from a number of locations in Rockland, including the Maine State Ferry Terminal and the Rockland Town Landing.

About 0.5 mile east of Rockland, several picnic tables are set up along US 1 in Glen Cove, courtesy of the Maine Department of Transportation. These invite visitors to stop, have lunch, and scan the cove for birds. The cove is almost bereft of water at extreme low tide.

11 Beech Hill Preserve

Habitats: Bald hilltop, organic blueberry fields, grasslands, mixed-hardwood forest.

Best time to bird: May through September. Snowy Owl have been reported here in winter. While chances are you won't see one of these, you may well see Wild Turkey and other common winter residents.

Nearest gas, food, and lodging: Rockland, Rockport, and Camden all have restaurants, inns, and motels. Gas is available along U.S. Route 1.

Nearest camping: Camden Hills State Park, Camden; (207) 236-3109 from May 1 through October 15 and (207) 236-0849 from October 16 through April 30. Megunticook Campground by the Sea, Rockport; (207) 594-2428.

For more information: Coastal Mountains Land Trust, 101 Mount Battie Street, Camden, ME 04843; (207) 236-7091; www.coastal mountains.org.

Directions: In Rockport drive south on US 1; turn right (west) onto Beech Hill Road, across from Hoboken Gardens. Drive for approximately 1 mile on Beech Hill Road, and look for a parking lot on the left, just past an old gate and stone fence. This takes you to Beech Hill Summit Road trailhead. *DeLorme: Maine Atlas and Gazetteer:* Page 14, D3

The birds

Look for Bobolink and Savannah Sparrow on the grasslands. Also present are Upland Sandpiper. Eastern Towhee inhabit the edges. American Kestrel and Northern Harrier glide over the grasslands. In 2006 Eastern Bluebird nested here in some swallow nesting boxes, an unexpected treat.

Besides the grassland birds, a great number of songbirds have been observed here. This includes 16 different warblers and 6 sparrow species in addition to Savannah Sparrow. Coastal Mountains Land Trust has compiled the *Beech Hill Preserve Bird List,* which lists 78 different species, including species seen or heard during bird surveys carried out in May and June 2006. The list also includes a few notable species recorded earlier.

About this site

The nearly 300-acre Beech Hill Preserve, a bastion of rural Maine set amid a rapidly changing landscape, was purchased in 2003 by Coastal Mountains Land Trust (CLT). While Beech Hill is a popular spot with local birders, CLT asks that large groups notify them before visiting the preserve. Since part of the preserve is dedicated to maintaining an organic blueberry operation (a process amenable to nesting birds), please do not stray off the trails.

Two trails have been established at the preserve. Summit Road Trail is an easy 0.75-mile walk with only a gradual incline. Make this your first choice for birding. The moderately difficult Woods Loop Trail winds through woods and along field edges.

In addition to scenic views, Beech Hill Preserve offers the chance to see a variety of grassland birds.

"Beech Nut," a sod-roofed stone hut, sits atop the summit and is listed on the National Register of Historic Places.

Nearby opportunities

Georges River Land Trust is in the process of building a hiking trail through the Georges River Watershed. Many sections of these trails offer good birding opportunities, plus some remarkable scenery. To learn more about the ongoing work of the Georges River Land Trust and some of their newer projects, contact them at 328 Main Street, Suite 305, Rockland, ME 04841; (207) 594-5166; e-mail grlt@midcoast.com.

⑫ Mount Battie

Habitats: Barren mountaintop; lots of mixed-growth forest on road to summit; stunted oak trees around edge of summit parking lot.

Best time to bird: In recent years, Turkey Vulture have arrived in this part of Maine as early as late March. Typically the vultures follow the retreating snowpack north. The springtime hawk migration begins in mid- to late April and lasts through much of May. The fall hawk migration begins in late September and continues into November. You can see Turkey Vulture riding the thermals at almost any time from spring through fall. The land-based birds are present around the summit edge and in the nearby woods from spring through fall. After the hawk migration ends in early November, there is not much to see until the following spring.

Nearest gas, food, and lodging: Camden is a tourist town and is filled with restaurants, motels, hotels, inns, and bed-and-breakfast establishments. Lincolnville Beach, a few miles north of Mount Battie, has several restaurants. U.S. Route 1, between Camden and Lincolnville Beach is lined with motels. Gas is available in Camden and along US 1.

Nearest camping: Camden Hills State Park, at the base of Mount Battie; (207) 236-3109 from May 1 through October 15 and (207) 236-0849 from October 16 through April 30. Megunticook Campground by the Sea, Rockport; (207) 594-2428.

For more information: Maine Bureau of Parks and Lands, 22 State House Station, Augusta, ME 04333; (207) 287-3821; www.maine.gov. For more on the trail to Bald Rock Mountain summit, see *Hiking Maine* (The Globe Pequot Press, 2002).

Directions: From Camden drive north on US 1. Look for the large wooden sign for Camden Hills State Park on the left, just on the outskirts of town. *DeLorme: Maine Atlas and Gazetteer:* Page 14, D4

The birds

Migrating hawks are the key birds here. Red-tailed, Broad-winged, and Sharp-shinned Hawk are in the majority. Also common are Northern Harrier, Merlin, and American Kestrel. Bald Eagle are often seen, as are Osprey and Turkey Vulture.

Look for Eastern Towhee and Brown Thrasher by the oaks around the parking lot.

About this site

Mount Battie is probably the best-known peak in Camden Hills State Park. An auto road (toll) makes it easy to reach the summit. Trails from Mount Battie lead through other sections of the park. Mount Battie offers startling views of Camden Harbor and Penobscot Bay. A small day-use fee is charged. Pick up a brochure and trail guide at the gate. Bring water and food if you plan to spend much time on a hawk watch.

The summit of Mount Battie attracts birders for the spring and fall hawk migrations.

Nearby opportunities

Across the road from Mount Battie is a seaside parcel of Camden Hills State Park. Here you can see a variety of gulls, Common Tern, and in winter, sea ducks. Bald Rock Mountain, in Lincolnville, another peak in Camden Hills State Park, offers a moderately strenuous hike to its peak. Bald Rock Mountain is another good site for watching migrating hawks. Laughing Gull sometimes frequent the harbor at Lincolnville Beach. Also at the beach, see a good variety of gulls. *DeLorme: Maine Atlas and Gazetteer:* Page 14, C4.

⑬ Passagassawakeag River

Habitats: Tidal river, exposed mudflats.

Best time to bird: While you will see gulls and terns in summer, most people head to the Passy in winter—anytime from November through March—to see the Barrow's Goldeneye.

Nearest gas, food, and lodging: Belfast is a tourist town and abounds in restaurants, motels, and bed-and-breakfasts. Gas is available along U.S. Route 1.

Nearest camping: Searsport Shores Camping Resort, US 1, 216 West Main Street, Searsport, ME 04974; (207) 548-6059; www.camp ocean.com.

For more information: City of Belfast; (207) 338-3370; www.cityofbelfast.org. Also see *Fishing Maine* (The Globe Pequot Press, 2007).

Directions: From points south of Belfast, drive north on US 1 to the intersection with Route 3 in Belfast. Turn right (east) here on the Belfast exit and head down Main Street to the Belfast waterfront. Turn left here onto Water Street, and park at the end of the Belfast Footbridge. *DeLorme: Maine Atlas and Gazetteer:* Page 14, A4

The new footbridge over the Passagassawakeag River in Belfast is a favorite spot for birders, especially in winter, when a wide variety of ducks are present.

The birds

The Passagassawakeag River, or "Passy," has long been noted as a place to visit in winter to watch for Barrow's Goldeneye, a key species here. Additionally, expect to see Common Goldeneye, American Black Duck, and Common Eider. This site hosts a mixed bag of gulls, including Glaucous, Iceland, and Bonaparte's. Common Tern are here in good numbers, too. Bald Eagle and Osprey often cruise the river, and a high-tension powerline near the river's head of tide holds an Osprey nest.

About this site

Birding could not be easier—a brand-new footbridge across the Passagassawakeag River opened to the public in 2006. The bridge allows birders to scan upriver and also gives a good view of Belfast Harbor. Boaters can launch at the Belfast Public Landing (for a fee) and head up the river, following the winding channel. Navigable water ends about 2 miles from town. A power line crosses the river at a narrow point, and in summer Double-crested Cormorant sit on the line.

Nearby opportunities

This is only a few miles from Moose Point State Park (see site 14). Just south of Belfast on US 1, Little River Harbor holds Bonaparte's Gull, Common Eider, and other seabirds.

⑭ Moose Point State Park

Habitats: Pine woods, mixed-growth successional forest, rocky ocean shore.

Best time to bird: Birding here is essentially productive year-round. May and early June are definitely good times to see migrating warblers. Summer visitors have plenty of opportunities, too, especially if you want to see Osprey and perhaps a Bald Eagle. Fall, September through November, brings migrating waterfowl. In winter Common Eider and other sea ducks swim in rafts not far from shore. Woodpeckers are present year-round. Look for signs of Pileated Woodpecker in the form of large, oblong holes on dead trees. Also look for piles of wood chips at the base of trees exhibiting woodpecker holes.

Nearest gas, food, and lodging: Belfast and Searsport offer restaurants, convenience stores, motels, inns, and bed-and-breakfasts.

Nearest camping: Searsport Shores Camping Resort, U.S. Route 1, 216 West Main Street, Searsport; (207) 548-6059; www.campocean .com.

For more information: Maine Bureau of Parks and Lands, 22 State House Station, Augusta, ME 04333-0022; (207) 548-2882 in-season, (207) 941-4014 off-season; www.maine.gov.

Directions: From Belfast head north on US 1. Immediately after crossing the Searsport town line, look for a large wooden sign on the right. Pull into the roadside parking lot and pay a small fee at a tollbooth, staffed only the warm weather. Or leave your be vehicle in the roadside parking lot and walk down into the park. Open fields lead downhill to the sea, and several signs point to the hiking trails on the right side of the fields. *DeLorme: Maine Atlas and Gazetteer:* Page 14, A5

The birds

In May the woodland trails at Moose Point are good spots to see migrating warblers, Hermit Thrush, Wood Thrush, and Veery. Additionally, look for year-round species here such as Black-capped Chickadee, Blue Jay, common crows, and ravens. Great Horned Owl and Barred Owl sometimes visit Moose Point, hunting for snowshoe hares and other small rodents. But the main attraction here is the rocky seashore. Here a variety of sea ducks are visible, as are Double-crested Cormorant, several kinds of gulls, Common Loon, Osprey, and the occasional Bald Eagle.

About this site

Moose Point, a small seaside jewel in Maine's state park system, lies about one-third of the way between Camden Hills State Park and Acadia National Park. It's one of those places that people heading for the better known parks routinely bypass. But that's their loss. Moose Point is never crowded and offers fine birding, as well as some hiking and picnicking.

Birding here is made easier by benches set here and there along the shore as well as along the gravel paths that lead through the successional forest. These provide a stable platform to sit and view birds through binoculars.

Visit Moose Point State Park's Woodland Trail in May for the spring warbler migration. Moose Point also offers seaside habitat and a variety of seabirds, gulls, and ducks.

Nearby opportunities

A few miles east of Moose Point in Searsport, Mossman Park and the Searsport Public Boat Landing present lots of opportunities for viewing seabirds. Once the author saw several Snow Goose feeding on the grounds at Mossman Park. The public landing has a long pier that extends well out into Penobscot Bay. This is a perfect place to scan the water for gulls, terns, sea ducks, and other waterfowl.
DeLorme: Maine Atlas and Gazetteer: Page 14, A5

15 Sears Island

Habitats: Sheltered cove on Penobscot Bay; also spruce/fir forests, mature oak forests, open fields, and reverting farmland; gravel clam flats exposed at low tide; a 941-acre, as-of-yet undeveloped, Maine island.

Best time to bird: November through March is prime times for wintering waterfowl. In spring, which can arrive as early as late March, songbirds return to the island's upland habitats. Summer is slow, except for gulls, eagles, and Osprey.

Nearest gas, food, and lodging: Searsport and Stockton Springs have restaurants, and there are motels and gas stations along U.S. Route 1 from Belfast to Prospect.

Nearest camping: Searsport Shores Camping Resort, US 1, 216 West Main Street, Searsport; (207) 548-6059; www.campocean.com.

For more information: Call the Town of Searsport at (207) 548-6372. Also see *Hiking Maine* (The Globe Pequot Press, 2002).

Directions: In Searsport drive east on US 1 for about 1.6 miles; look for Sears Island Road to the right (east), near a small green building. This is almost directly across US 1 from a highway department salt and sand shed. Turn right (east) and follow this road. Cross a railroad track and drive out onto the causeway. The causeway ends at a concrete barrier at the entrance to the island, about 1.5 miles from US 1. *DeLorme: Maine Atlas and Gazetteer:* Page 15, A1

The birds

In winter birders frequent the causeway that separates Sears Island from the mainland. If it's uncomfortably cold, you can watch wintering waterfowl from the warmth of a parked, heated vehicle. At high tide, especially, you can get close-up views of Pie-billed and Horned Grebe, Common Goldeneye, Bufflehead, American Black Duck, Common Loon, and occasionally Barrow's Goldeneye. Bald Eagle frequent the island and are often seen near the causeway.

The island itself is a mix of wetlands, fields, edge habitat, and upland forests, mostly fir and spruce. Ruffed Grouse and American Woodcock are common here; common crows, ravens, and Blue Jay are also present. In spring walk the island trails for migrating warblers.

About this site

The causeway is a favorite site for local birders. There are numerous places along the causeway to pull off the road and park while you scan the cove. Publicly owned Sears Island is at the center of a continuing controversy as to whether to save it intact or to allow some kind of commercial or industrial development. Even if the island is developed, a major portion will be set aside for public use.

Hikers flock to the island, and it is possible to spend an entire day hiking and enjoying nature. This site is highly recommended for families with children.

Near this sandy beach on Sears Island, birders can sit in their vehicles while parked on the causeway and scan the sea for Bald Eagle, Osprey, gulls, and sea ducks.

Nearby opportunities

At Fort Point Cove, on the north side of Cape Jellison (easily viewed from Sears Island), you can see many of the same waterfowl species as at Sears Island. However, Fort Point Cove also hosts Ruddy Duck. These can be seen from Cape Jellison Road, on the north end of the cape, and from the fishing pier at Fort Point State Park. *DeLorme: Maine Atlas and Gazetteer:* Page 15, A2

16 James Dorso Wildlife Management Area— Ruffingham Meadow

Habitats: Inland wetland, mixed forestland, successional edge growth, some fields.

Best time to bird: Springtime, the month of May in particular, sees considerable bird activity at Dorso WMA. June is also a good month to see groups of ducks paddling about. This can be done from the road, at the gravel parking area along Route 3. The fall migration, from September through October, is another good time. Bald Eagle may be seen here at any time of year.

Nearest gas, food, and lodging: In Liberty a motel and several restaurants offer food and lodging. Otherwise drive east to Belfast for food, lodging, and gas.

Nearest camping: Cozy Pines Campground, Montville; (207) 589-4750. Lake St. George State Park, Liberty; (207) 589-4255.

For more information: Maine Department of Inland Fisheries and Wildlife, 284 State Street, 41 State House Station, Augusta, ME 04333-0041; (207) 287-8000; www.mefish wildlife.com.

Directions: From the intersection of U.S. Route 1 and Route 3 in Belfast, drive west on Route 3 for about 12 miles to North Searsmont. Look for a sign and a gravel parking lot by a pond and wetland on the right (north) side of the road. *DeLorme: Maine Atlas and Gazetteer:* Page 14, B2

The birds

Ducks flock to Dorso Wildlife Management Area (WMA) for the wild rice planted for them by the State of Maine. Look for Wood Duck, American Black Duck, Blue-winged Teal, Green-winged Teal, Mallard, and Hooded Merganser. According to the Maine Department of Inland Fisheries and Wildlife, the late James Dorso, the WMA's namesake, established a viable breeding population of Common Goldeneye. Dorso introduced these ducks here from other areas, and now they nest at this WMA every spring.

Other birds of interest include American Bittern, Least Bittern, Belted Kingfisher, Canada Goose, and Sora Rail. Upland portions of the WMA host American Woodcock, Ruffed Grouse, and Wild Turkey.

About this site

The 610-acre Ruffingham Meadow WMA was formed when Maine's Department of Inland Fisheries and Wildlife impounded Bartlett Stream. A small pond quickly formed, and the balance of the impoundment became wetland. This soon attracted ducks, and Ruffingham Meadow became a prime destination for waterfowl hunters and later, for birders.

A small, gravel parking area and rough boat landing alongside Route 3 can accommodate five or six vehicles. Much of the open-water section of the WMA

James Dorso Wildlife Management Area in spring. Later this impoundment will be filled with wild rice—and lots of waterfowl.

can be scanned from the road, but a canoe permits fuller exploration. Paddling the length of the pond, you will find a maze of channels, many of them cul-de-sacs, at the head of the pond. The main stem, Bartlett Brook, has the greatest flow and is deeper than the others. The canoe trip here is worth at least several hours; to really get to know this WMA, plan to spend at least half a day. Paddling through tall-growing wild rice with bird life all around is truly a memorable experience.

Nearby opportunities

The Frye Mountain WMA lies about 5 miles north of James Dorso WMA. Once-derelict apple orchards have been "freed," or pruned and opened, to provide habitat for Ruffed Grouse and American Woodcock. Warblers and other songbirds can be seen in the successional and edge habitat along the many fields at this WMA, and Wild Turkey are literally everywhere. To reach Frye Mountain WMA from James Dorso WMA, drive west on Route 3 to Liberty. Turn right (north) onto Route 220 and travel about 7 miles. Turn right (east) onto Walker Ridge Road. Drive about 2 miles, bearing right at the first two-way intersection, to a sign marking the beginning of State of Maine land and Frye Mountain WMA.

⑰ Sandy Point Wildlife Management Area— Stowers Meadow

Habitats: Inland freshwater marsh and meadow, small pond, alder swales around edges, some mixed-growth upland forest.

Best time to bird: The spring migration ranks high. Come in mid-May, and after checking out the open-water section, take a walk through the upland area to the left of the access road. Summertime also presents lots of waterbird opportunities. Good birding ends with the fall migration.

Nearest gas, food, and lodging: Stockton Springs has a restaurant, several convenience stores, and a motel. U.S. Route 1 between Belfast and Stockton Springs is lined with restaurants, motels, and bed-and-breakfasts.

Nearest camping: Searsport Shores Camping Resort, US 1, 216 West Maine Street, Searsport; (207) 548-6059; www.campocean.com.

For more information: Maine Department of Inland Fisheries and Wildlife, 284 State Street, 41 State House Station, Augusta, ME 04333-0041; (207) 287-8000; www.mefish wildlife.com.

Directions: In Stockton Springs head north (east) on US 1 to the village of Sandy Point. Continue on US 1 for 0.8 mile, drive under a railroad overpass, and turn left onto Muskrat Road on the immediate left (west), just past the overpass. The road to Sandy Point WMA is the first road on the right; look for a sign for Sandy Point WMA by the entrance. Drive down this road and park near the dam. Note that the road is somewhat rough, and can have deep mud puddles in spring and after summer rains. *DeLorme: Maine Atlas and Gazetteer:* Page 23, E2

The birds

Sandy Point WMA is loaded with Ring-necked Duck and American Bittern. This is a key destination for anyone who wants to see, not just hear, an American Bittern. Also present are Least Bittern and Pied-billed Grebe. In years past this WMA supported the largest colony of Least Bittern found in Maine. Additionally, Sandy Point hosts a large population of Sora Rail as well as some Virginia Rail. Great Blue Heron frequent this shallow impoundment. Osprey also frequent the impounded area, offering close-up views as they hunt for fish. Common Grackle, Red-winged Blackbird, and Marsh Wren all find a home here.

Belted Kingfisher haunt the stream below the dam. Often they are seen sitting on the metal rail at the dam. Ruffed Grouse, Wild Turkey, and American Woodcock inhabit the uplands surrounding the wetland. Common Snipe inhabit the riparian habitat.

Waterbirds abound here, including Green-winged and Blue-winged Teal, Wood Duck, and Hooded Merganser.

Bald Eagle are always a possibility here.

Sparsely visited Sandy Point Wildlife Management Area is one of Maine's better places to see and hear American Bittern.

About this site

As is the case with so many other WMAs, this site remains undeveloped. A rough, clay-bottomed road leads to the dam at the foot of the impoundment, where you can easily scan most open-water areas. Locals launch their canoes to the left of the dam.

Prior to becoming a state-owned WMA, this place was called "The Muskrat Farm," for the commercial fur business located here. In addition to the very fine birding possibilities, a small population of native brook trout inhabits the impoundment.

Nearby opportunities

The town of Stockton Springs manages a 100-acre park, Sandy Point Beach State Park, in the little seaside community of Sandy Point, about 0.8 mile south of Sandy Point WMA. A newly completed 1.5-mile hiking trail winds through upland woodlands and up on a sandy beach. A portion of this hiking trail is wheelchair accessible. Look for songbirds and upland gamebirds in the upland habitat. Waterfowl and gulls are present on this wide cove on the Penobscot River.

18 Howard L. Mendall Wildlife Management Area—Sandy Stream

Habitats: Tidal wetlands, mudflats; open water on Marsh Stream, a tidal stream.

Best time to bird: Look for migrating waterfowl from late September through October. Often large flights of Common Snipe set down on the wetlands. American Black Duck congregate in tidal pools, and shorebirds walk the mudflats at low tide. Look for these in fall. Rails are present throughout summer and into October. Osprey, Bald Eagle, and Herring Gull may be seen year-round.

Nearest gas, food, and lodging: Look for a restaurant in Stockton Springs, as well a motel. Motels, restaurants, as gas are plentiful on U.S. Route 1A from Hampden to Bangor.

Nearest camping: Paul Bunyan Campground, Bangor; (207) 941-1177. Pleasant Hill RV Park and Campground, Bangor; (207) 848-5127.

For more information: Maine Department of Inland Fisheries and Wildlife, 284 State Street, 41 State House Station, Augusta, ME 04333-0041; (207) 287-8000; www.mefishwildlife.com.

Directions: From Stockton Springs head north on US 1A. After about 9.2 miles look for a sign on the right-hand (east) side of the road for Howard L. Mendall Wildlife Management Area Unit and a rough gravel road leading through the marsh and to the edge of Marsh Stream. *DeLorme: Maine Atlas and Gazetteer:* Page 23, E1

The birds

A key bird, Nelson's Sharp-tailed Sparrow, breeds at Mendall Marsh. Other birds of interest include Common Merganser, Sora and Virginia Rail, Common Snipe, Least Sandpiper, Semipalmated Sandpiper, and Greater and Lesser Yellowlegs. Osprey and Bald Eagle are often present out over the stream, as are a variety of ducks, Common Loon, and Canada Goose. Several kinds of sparrows inhabit the low growth along the access road.

About this site

Sandy Stream is managed by the Maine Department of Inland Fisheries and Wildlife. The marsh is composed mostly of short grasses, and although it looks as though you couldn't walk on it, the surface is amazingly firm. However, little narrow tidal channels weave their way throughout the marsh and are often obscured by vegetation. Use extreme caution as you walk the marsh—the channels are often several feet or more deep.

The marsh is in a completely natural state—there are no facilities here of any kind.

Birders at Mendall Marsh often find tracks of shorebirds as they walk the river's edge at low tide.

Nearby opportunities

The public boat launch on Verona Island is a good place to walk about in winter and scan the Penobscot River for Barrow's Goldeneye. *DeLorme: Maine Atlas and Gazetteer:* Page 23, E2

Down East Maine

Down East Maine, noted for quiet ocean coves, lighthouses, and working fishing communities, has a mostly untapped potential as a birder's paradise. Seabirds, shorebirds, and birds more likely to be seen in northern forests are all here. Down East Maine is a magnet for migrating springtime warblers—a migration that has only recently begun to attract tourists.

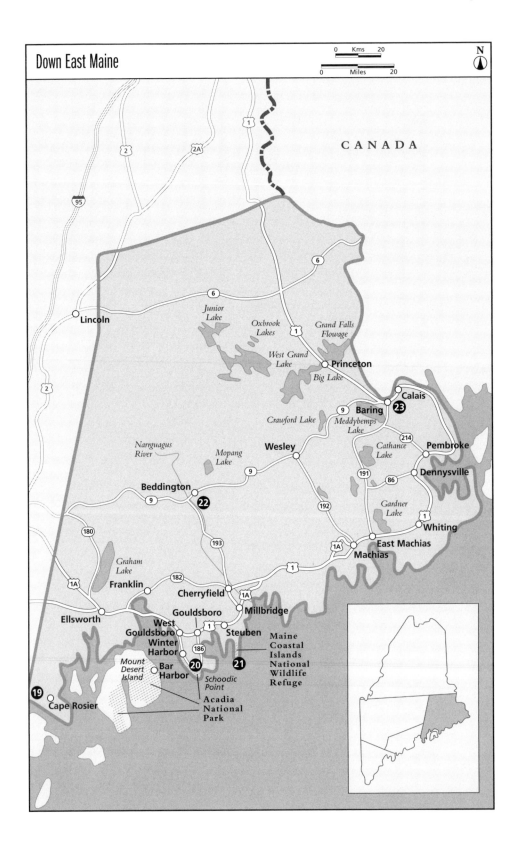

Down East Maine

CANADA

Lincoln

Junior Lake
Oxbrook Lakes
Grand Falls Flowage
West Grand Lake
Princeton
Big Lake

Calais **23**
Baring
Crawford Lake
Meddybemps Lake
Cathance Lake
Pembroke
Dennysville

Narraguagus River
Mopang Lake
Wesley

Beddington **22**

Gardner Lake
Whiting

Graham Lake

East Machias
Machias

Franklin
Cherryfield
Millbridge

Ellsworth

Gouldsboro
West Gouldsboro
Winter Harbor
Steuben

Mount Desert Island
Bar Harbor **20**
21

Schoodic Point

Acadia National Park

Maine Coastal Islands National Wildlife Refuge

19
Cape Rosier

19 Holbrook Island Sanctuary

Habitats: Freshwater wetlands, fields, spruce-fir forest, reverting farmland, saltwater marsh, and a protected, saltwater cove on Penobscot Bay.

Best time to bird: Year-round.

Access: While some areas of the sanctuary require a bit of uphill hiking, others are accessible from a motor vehicle. The sanctuary headquarters is located on a grassy hill near the sea, and here visitors may see seabirds as well as a variety of landbirds. Sanctuary roads wind past freshwater marshes, and you can pull to the side of the road and scan the area for birds.

Nearest gas, food, and lodging: Brooksville and South Brooksville have variety stores that sell food and fuel. Lodging is available in nearby Blue Hill, Orland, and Bucksport.

Nearest camping: Masthead Campground, Bucksport; (207) 469-3482. Shady Oaks Campground & Cabins, Orland; (207) 469-7739. Balsam Cove Campground, East Orland; (800) 469-7771.

For more information: Holbrook Island Sanctuary, 172 Indian Bar Road, Brooksville, ME 04617; (207) 326-4012; www.maine.gov/doc/parks.

Directions: At the intersection of Cape Rosier and Back Roads, on Cape Rosier, turn west (right), on Back Road where a sign reads ENTERING HOLBROOK ISLAND SANCTUARY. Drive 2.4 miles to Mountain Loop trailhead, where you will find a small parking place and a box on a post filled with information leaflets and maps of the sanctuary. *DeLorme: Maine Atlas and Gazetteer:* Page 15, B2

The birds

You should easily see or hear the following waterfowl common to Holbrook Island in the course of a day's birding: Common Loon, Horned Grebe, Canada Goose, Blue-winged Teal, Long-tailed Duck, Surf Scoter, White-winged Scoter, Common Goldeneye, Bufflehead, and Red-breasted Merganser.

Several different shorebirds are usually present at low tide, including Black-bellied Plover, Semipalmated Plover, and Least Sandpiper. In addition to Herring Gull, look for Bonaparte's and Great Black-backed Gull. Black Guillemot are visible from shore at various points along Holbrook's shoreline.

Breeding birds at Holbrook Island include, but are not limited to, Double-crested Cormorant, Great Blue Heron, Common Eider, Osprey, and Bald Eagle. Holbrook also has a long list of songbirds common to the preserve.

Some birds are rare or uncommon visitors to Holbrook Island. Among these are Red-throated Loon, Red-necked Grebe, Northern Gannet, Great Cormorant, Snowy Egret, Green-backed Heron, Black-crowned Night Heron, Snow Goose, Brant, King Eider, Harlequin Duck, and Barrow's Goldeneye. Other uncommon visitors are Solitary, Western, White-rumped, Baird's, Pectoral, and Purple Sandpiper; Red-Necked Phalarope; Common Black-headed Gull; and Roseate Tern.

Besides freshwater wetlands, Holbrook Island Sanctuary features lots of upland habitat, ocean shoreline, even a small mountain.

The list of uncommon visitors ends with Black-billed and Yellow-billed Cuckoo, Short-eared Owl, Black-backed Woodpecker, Gray Jay, and Boreal Chickadee. There is no guarantee birders will see any of these uncommon visitors, but the chance exists.

The varied types of habitat at Holbrook Island Sanctuary account for the great diversity of bird species. Since shorebirds, waterfowl, warblers, and birds more typical of the northern forest are found here, birders can enjoy their hobby year-round, with every expectation of seeing enough different kinds of birds to make their visit a profitable one.

In May the warbler migration attracts birders. Later in spring and in early summer nesting waterfowl and shorebirds are prominent. In summer the hiking trails at Holbrook can reward visitors with sightings of northern forest birds. And in fall, winter, and early spring, birders are rewarded with not only many common ducks and other types of waterfowl but also several uncommon species.

About this site

Holbrook Island Sanctuary is managed as a nature and wildlife sanctuary, rather than as a park. Holbrook Island has well-maintained hiking trails, picnic tables, and considerable shore frontage, but the real stars are the plants and animals. The sanctuary's 1,350-acres were donated to the people of the State of Maine by former landowner Anita Harris.

The Maine State Department of Conservation, Bureau of Parks and Lands, manages the sanctuary along with the Holbrook Island Sanctuary Corporation. The Friends of Holbrook Island, part of that corporation, manages the sanctuary in accordance with Anita Harris's wishes that the land remain: " . . . forever wild as a bit of wilderness in an inhabited region, devoted wholly to the preservation of nature—animal, bird and plant life . . . " The organization hosts a variety of educational programs throughout the year.

A birder can easily spend a whole day here, given the varied terrain and different kinds of habitat. Some things to keep in mind, though, are that since the sanctuary is situated on a point of land at the head of Penobscot Bay, cold winds can buffet the place any time of year, including the summer months. Always bring warm clothing. Also, since fog often blows in from the sea, a rain jacket or nylon windbreaker is advised. And with its salt and freshwater marshes, Holbrook Island Sanctuary has a generous supply of mosquitoes. In May and June blackflies are present in numbers, especially on inland parts of the sanctuary. Insect repellent is a must.

Since Holbrook Island is truly "off the beaten path," it sees few visitors compared to other locations in Maine's state park system. A day spent here birding may well be one spent in solitude.

Nearby opportunities

A drive around Cape Rosier offers both spectacular scenery and opportunities to see a variety of seabirds.

20 Schoodic Point

Habitats: Rocky point at the end of a long peninsula facing out into the Gulf of Maine.

Best time to bird: Schoodic Point offers rewarding birding possibilities year-round. Expect to see eagles, Common Loon, scoters, Common Eider, Black Guillemot, and Great Black-backed Gull whenever you visit. In winter look for Purple Sandpiper, Harlequin Duck, and Barrow's Goldeneye. If you are to see a King Eider, it will be in winter. Auks, or Razorbill, also spend the winter off Schoodic Point.

Nearest gas, food, and lodging: Food is available in Winter Harbor. For a wider variety of food choices, as well as for more places to stay and refuel, return to Ellsworth.

Nearest camping: Acadia National Park; do call ahead for reservations. Mount Desert Island also has numerous privately owned campgrounds.

For more information: Acadia National Park; (207) 288-3338; www.nps.gov/acad. Also see *Hiking Maine* (The Globe Pequot Press, 2002) and *Maine Off the Beaten Path* (The Globe Pequot Press, 2006).

Directions: From Ellsworth head east on U.S. Route 1 and continue to West Gouldsboro. Turn right (south) onto Route 186 to Winter Harbor. In Winter Harbor follow signs to the Acadia National Park entrance and the one-way loop road that will take you around Schoodic Peninsula and to land's end at Schoodic Point. *DeLorme: Maine Atlas and Gazetteer:* Page 17, C1

The birds

Waterfowl, gulls, and a variety of seabirds attract birders to this pristine location. Look for Surf, White-winged, and Black Scoter. Common Eider are present, and King Eider are a possibility. Watch the rocks along water's edge for Purple Sandpiper. Harlequin Duck, and Barrow's Goldeneye are present, too. And always there is a chance that a Bald Eagle will pass by, lending a finishing touch to your day of birding.

About this site

Schoodic Point is part of Acadia National Park, one of a number of units of the park not situated directly upon Mount Desert Island (MDI). The 6-mile one-way road that takes you all the way around Schoodic Peninsula, and to Schoodic Point at the peninsula's very end, does not see anywhere near as much traffic as do park roads on MDI. It is still possible to witness awe-inspiring scenery all by yourself.

A quick glance at any map will show that Schoodic Point extends a far distance out into the ocean. That happy occurrence, of course, is what draws the great variety of birds here.

Be sure to bring plenty of food and water, since the town of Winter Harbor is about the last chance to find any kind of supplies. That said, plan to spend a day birding, lounging, and enjoying this natural wonder to the fullest.

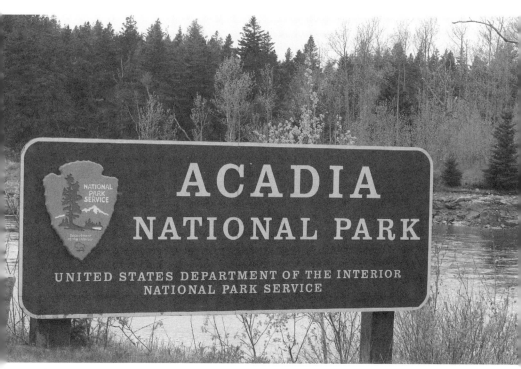

This sign welcomes visitors to the rocky, surf-tossed Schoodic Peninsula. From Schoodic Point, birders can view birds that inhabit the Gulf of Maine.

Nearby opportunities

Schoodic Head, a 440-foot mountain on Schoodic Peninsula, offers not only a scenic and somewhat exhilarating hike but also lots of birding possibilities. Schoodic Head is a fairly reliable site for Spruce Grouse. A good variety of songbirds are present, including a few boreal varieties. To reach Schoodic Head, continue just a short distance past the Schoodic Point and look for a turnout and sign for the trailhead on the left. The road here is one-way (counterclockwise), leading back to Route 186.

㉑ Petit Manan Point, Maine Coastal Islands National Wildlife Refuge

Habitats: This long, narrow peninsula extends out toward the Gulf of Maine. On it are blueberry barrens, marshes, spruce forests, mixed-growth forest, cedar swamps, raised heath peatlands, stands of jack pine, successional habitat on field edges, freshwater and saltwater marshes, granite shoreline, and cobble beaches.

Best time to bird: Good birding can be had year-round at Petit Manan Point. The spring waterfowl migration begins in late March and continues through mid-May. Summer is when nesting seabirds and songbirds rear their young. In mid-July shorebirds arrive on their southward migration (if this seems early, remember how far these birds must travel). In fall, September through November, raptors, waterfowl, and songbirds migrate. Sea ducks form large rafts offshore, and Peregrine Falcon, Sharp-shinned Hawk, and Merlin can be seen as they follow the twisting shoreline on their southward migration. Winter is prime time for walking the trails and looking for

Boreal Chickadee and Spruce Grouse. Snowy Owl sometimes make the trek here from their homes in the Canadian tundra. Winter is also a great time to scan the sea for seabirds, and you may see some uncommon sea ducks, perhaps even Harlequin, Barrow's Goldeneye, and King Eider. Even if you don't see any of these, you will encounter a good variety of seabirds.

Nearest gas, food, and lodging: Restaurants and take-out services are available along U.S. Route 1 between Gouldsboro and Milbridge. More services, including motels and gas stations, are available in Ellsworth and Machias.

Nearest camping: McLellan Park, Millbridge.

For more information: Maine Coastal Islands Wildlife Refuge, P.O. Box 279, Water Street, Millbridge, ME 04658; (207) 546-2124. You can also get information from the U.S. Fish and Wildlife Service; (800) 344-9453; www.fws.gov. Be sure and ask either of these agencies for the brochure *Maine Coastal Islands National Wildlife Refuge, Birds.*

Directions: From Gouldsboro and points south, head east on US 1 to Steuben. In Steuben look for Pigeon Hill Road on the right. Take Pigeon Hill Road and drive south for 5.8 miles to the parking area for Birch Point Trail on Petit Manan Point. *DeLorme: Maine Atlas and Gazetteer:* Page 17, A3 and B3

The birds

The complete list of key birds, too extensive to include here, is available at no charge from refuge headquarters. However, that only points out the great number of bird species seen here. Highlights include Hermit and Swainson's Thrush, Song Sparrow, and various warblers, including Nashville, Magnolia, Palm, and Black-throated Green Warbler. Also expect to see Boreal Chickadee in the forested areas.

Shorebirds seen along the mudflats can include Semipalmated, Least, and several other species of sandpiper; Black-bellied Plover; Short-billed Dowitcher; Greater and Lesser Yellowlegs; and Dunlin.

Ducks flock to Cranberry Flowage in fall, and these will include American Black Duck, Green-winged Teal, Mallard, and Northern Pintail. As many as 4,000 ducks have been recorded at one time in this 80-acre flowage.

Grassland birds nesting on the overgrown pastureland on Petit Manan Point include Bobolink and Savannah Sparrow.

Looking out to sea from Petit Manan Point, you can expect to see Common Eider and Surf Scoter, a variety of gulls, Bald Eagle, and Osprey. Again, these are only a few of what you may see here at different times.

About this site

Petit Manan Point is only one part of a larger system, which includes both coastal parcels and offshore islands. The system ranges over 200 miles of Maine's rocky coast and comprises more than 7,000 acres.

The Petit Manan Point Division is included here for several reasons. One is the staggering array of bird species that either live here year-round, nest here and move on, or stop by on their migration routes. Second, Petit Manan Point is easily accessible, is open year-round, and has excellent foot trails that lead through a wide variety of habitats. Interpretive signs are placed at key points along the trails. Maps and brochures are available at the trailhead.

While Petit Manan Point is mostly known for its undeveloped seashore, this remote peninsula also features freshwater wetlands, fields, and upland habitat.

While the refuge system's seabird islands are closed to the public during nesting season, Maine Coastal Islands National Wildlife Refuge is open year-round during daylight hours. Be aware that not all of Petit Manan Point is part of the national wildlife refuge. Private property is well marked, though.

NOTE: Activities not permitted at many other sites are allowed at this national wildlife refuge. You may hand-pick blueberries and harvest shellfish in accordance with state and local regulations.

Nearby opportunities

McLellan Park, a scenic town-owned park on the rocky headland along Narraguagus Bay, offers some of the most striking scenery found in Washington County, including lots of wild ocean and offshore islands. Many of the birds present at Petit Manan Point will be found here, too. Trails winding along the rocks often open to wide ocean vistas where you can scan for seabirds. Other trails wind through the sparse shrubs and mixed-growth habitat, perfect for a springtime warbler walk. The ruggedness of the terrain, though, demands extra caution at all times. Picnic tables and campsites (stop at the Millbridge Town Office for a camping permit) round out the offerings. Whatever you do here, bring a camera in order to capture some of the stunning ocean views and hopefully interesting birds. To reach McLellan Park from Steuben, head east on US 1 and continue to the town of Millbridge. Just as you get into town, look for Wyman Road on the right (east) on a sharp curve on US 1. Take Wyman Road and drive about 4 miles and look for a sign on the left for McLellan Park. *DeLorme: Maine Atlas and Gazetteer:* Page 17, A3

22 Bog Brook Wildlife Management Area

Habitats: A 924-acre impounded wetland complex (part of a 1,600-acre wetland) with riparian habitat consisting of emergent growth. Lots of flooded timber in impoundment. Near to commercial blueberry land and barrens.

Best time to bird: Spring migration has much to recommend it. Try visiting in May and June. However, the large fish-eating birds are present from spring through fall, as are the waterfowl, making any time from mid-May until early November worthwhile times to visit.

Nearest gas, food, and lodging: Brewer, at the beginning of Route 9, has plenty of restaurants and motels. Also find motels, restaurants, gas, and general stores on U.S. Route 1 between Cherryfield and Machias.

Nearest camping: Greenwood Acres Campground, Route 178, Eddington; (888) 989-8898. Mainayr Campground, 321 Village Road, Steuben; (207) 546-2690.

For more information: Maine Department of Inland Fisheries and Wildlife, 284 State Street, 41 State House Station, Augusta, ME 04333-0041; (207) 287-8000; www.mefishwildlife.com.

Directions: From the Hancock–Washington County border (intersection of Routes 9 and 193), drive east on Route 9 (aka The Airline) for about 0.5 mile. This takes you over the Narraguagus River. Turn right (south) onto the first road immediately past the river, and continue driving south for about 2 miles to where the road forks. Turn right (south) at the fork, and drive another 4 miles to a little wooden bridge. Turn left immediately after crossing the bridge. This leads you to the outlet dam and a small parking area. The dam, by the way, is visible from the bridge. *DeLorme: Maine Atlas and Gazetteer:* Page 25, B2

The birds

Great Blue Heron, Osprey, and Bald Eagle nest here, making Bog Brook Wildlife Management Area (WMA) a vitally important site. These large fish-eating birds are attracted by the flooded, dead timber, where fish commonly seek shade and shelter.

The impoundment hosts Common Loon, American Black Duck, Hooded Merganser, Wood Duck, and Ring-necked Duck. Common Snipe and Spotted Sandpiper frequent the edge habitat, and Northern Harrier fly over the impoundment. Red-winged Blackbird and Common Grackle sit in the shrubs alongside the impoundment, and Tree Swallow dart about, picking mosquitoes and blackflies out of the air.

About this site

Bog Brook WMA, like so many other prime birding sites in Maine, is owned and managed by the Maine Department of Inland Fisheries and Wildlife (DIF&W). A small parking lot by the dam/outlet offers room for several vehicles. There are absolutely no facilities at this wild, somewhat remote site.

Bog Brook Wildlife Management Area hosts Bald Eagles, Osprey, shorebirds, and myriad water-fowl. Only a handful of birders visit this remote, semiwild site.

While you can stand or sit near the dam and scan the impoundment (binoculars or a spotting scope will help), the most exciting way to investigate Bog Brook WMA is by canoe. You can easily launch your canoe by the dam and paddle up either side of this winding, convoluted shoreline.

Note that while DIF&W owns the WMA, a limited section of the access road crosses commercially managed blueberry land. For a number of reasons, including visitor safety, the company asks that visitors call (207) 546-2311 in order to secure permission to use the private road.

Nearby opportunities

Another reason to call ahead is to combine a trip through the vast blueberry barrens with your visit to Bog Brook WMA. To reach the barrens (thousands of wide-open, undulating, boulder-strewn acres managed for commercial blueberry production), you can continue south after crossing the little wooden bridge near the WMA outlet. The WMA is bounded by the barrens. It's about 10 miles between Bog Brook WMA and Cherryfield, the first town to the south.

Upland Sandpiper and Vesper Sparrow nest here, and driving down the road early and late in the day in May and June can result in lots of roadside sightings. Also look for Horned Lark, Eastern Meadowlark, Bobolink, and Eastern Towhee. In May the barrens hold numbers of migrating warblers. All in all, a drive through Maine's Down East blueberry barrens is a great treat for birders.

A few suggestions are in order: First, although the general public makes regular use of them, these are private roads. Company trucks have the right-of-way, and you must always be prepared to yield. Also, never pick blueberries here—they are a private, commercial crop. It's best to stay in your car while birding or, at the least, to pull aside and scan the barrens from the roadside. It is easy to become disoriented and even lost on this vast inland plain.

㉓ Moosehorn National Wildlife Refuge, Baring Division

Habitats: Marshes, forests, streams, ponds, fields, edge habitat, and successional vegetation.

Best time to bird: Birding opportunities abound year-round. Beginning in early April American Woodcock pour into Moosehorn to conduct their acrobatic courtship flights each day at dusk and dawn. This aerial ballet lasts about 30 minutes. Mating season continues through mid-May, at which time refuge wetlands come alive with waterfowl, wading birds, and shorebirds. Many of these birds come here to breed; others use Moosehorn as a stop along their northward trek to breeding grounds farther north.

June brings a new scene, with ducks and geese and their broods walking about along Magurrewock Marsh, near U.S. Route 1. Also now, eagles and Osprey tend their young in nests built upon specially constructed nesting platforms.

Later in summer, Great Blue Heron and American Bittern are in evidence, as are a great variety of songbirds. In all, 220 species of birds have been documented in Moosehorn National Wildlife Refuge.

At all times of the year, forested areas of the refuge host boreal species. Look for Boreal Chickadee, Gray Jay, and Spruce Grouse.

Nearest gas, food, and lodging: The city of Calais, on the U.S.–Canada border, is filled with restaurants, stores, gas stations, motels, and bed-and-breakfasts.

Nearest camping: Cobscook Bay State Park, US 1, Dennysville; (207) 726-4412; www.campwithme.com.

For more information: Moosehorn National Wildlife Refuge, RR 1, Box 202, Suite 1, Baring, ME 04694-9759; (207) 454-7161; www.fws.gov/northeast/moosehorn. The refuge office is open Monday through Friday, 7:30 a.m. to 4:00 p.m.

Directions: From Calais head southwest on US 1. Immediately after leaving the built-up section of the city, look for Magurrewock Marsh on both sides of the road. The highway here is built on a dike. Look for a large National Wildlife Refuge sign on the left (south) side of the road, just after you cross the dike. Follow that road to the refuge headquarters. *DeLorme: Maine Atlas and Gazetteer:* Page 36, C5

The birds

One of the most northern national wildlife refuges on the Atlantic Flyway, Moosehorn is an important nesting and feeding site for waterfowl. Wading birds, shorebirds, upland birds, Bald Eagle, and Osprey nest here, dependent upon the Baring Division's 17,200-acres of prime habitat.

Besides all this, 23 species of warblers nest at Moosehorn. Also, Moosehorn is intensely managed to produce and maintain habitat for American Woodcock.

This wheelchair-accessible observation deck at Moosehorn National Wildlife Refuge is a great site to set up a camera and tripod.

About this site

Moosehorn National Wildlife Refuge was established in 1937 to serve as a refuge and breeding area for migratory birds and other wildlife. More than 50 miles of refuge roads and trails are closed to vehicular traffic but open to hiking, cross-country skiing, and of course birding. Black bears, white-tailed deer, moose, otters, and beavers are also in evidence. Trail and road maps are available at refuge head-quarters in Baring.

Two wheelchair-accessible observation decks (during times of bare ground) allow for bird and wildlife viewing. These and other prime spots are often visited by professional and nonprofessional wildlife photographers. Here is a perfect chance to get a great shot of a nesting Bald Eagle.

Wildlife biologists conduct regular woodcock and waterfowl banding opera-tions, and the public is invited to participate. Call ahead to schedule your trip. Free tours, programs, and nature walks, as well as an annual warbler walk, are hosted throughout the summer. Schedules are available from refuge headquarters.

Self-guided tours are available on well-maintained refuge trails. The Woodcock Trail, a self-interpreting, wheelchair-accessible trail, winds through a quarter mile of specially designed woodcock habitat.

The Raven Trail leads through a diverse assortment of wildlife habitat, including forests, along Dudley Swamp, and through managed cuts. This presents an easy way to view songbirds as well as birds of prey. Both trails begin at refuge headquarters.

Nearby opportunities

While the Baring Division is the larger and perhaps the most diverse of the refuge's two divisions, the 7,189-acre Edmunds Division of Moosehorn National Wildlife Refuge covers several miles of shoreline on Dennys Bay. Gulls, terns, accipers, and shorebirds are only some of what makes this a worthwhile place to visit. This division has upland habitat as well and, like the Baring Division, contains a National Wilderness Area. The Edmunds Division is located on US 1 between Whiting and Dennysville, across the road from Cobscook Bay State Park. *DeLorme: Maine Atlas and Gazetteer:* Page 27, A1

Another nearby site is well worth visiting. Orange River Wildlife Management Area (WMA), 1 mile west of Whiting Village on US 1, is a 588-acre impounded freshwater wetland. This is an excellent waterfowl and shorebird site. Birds of interest here include Pied-billed Grebe, Hooded Merganser, Ring-necked Duck, American Bittern, Least Bittern, and Virginia Rail. For more information on Orange River WMA, contact Maine Department of Inland Fisheries and Wildlife, 284 State Street, 41 State House Station, Augusta, ME 04333-0041; (207) 287-8000; www.mefishwildlife.com. *DeLorme: Maine Atlas and Gazetteer:* Page 27, B1

Central Maine

entral Maine is a region of open farm country, lakes, streams, bogs, and dense forests. It is a place where northern and southern ranges of many birds, plants, and animals meet. Several of Maine's medium-size cities are located here, but even in cities birders have many fine opportunities. Eagles and Osprey fly up and down the Penobscot and Kennebec Rivers, providing many thrilling birding opportunities.

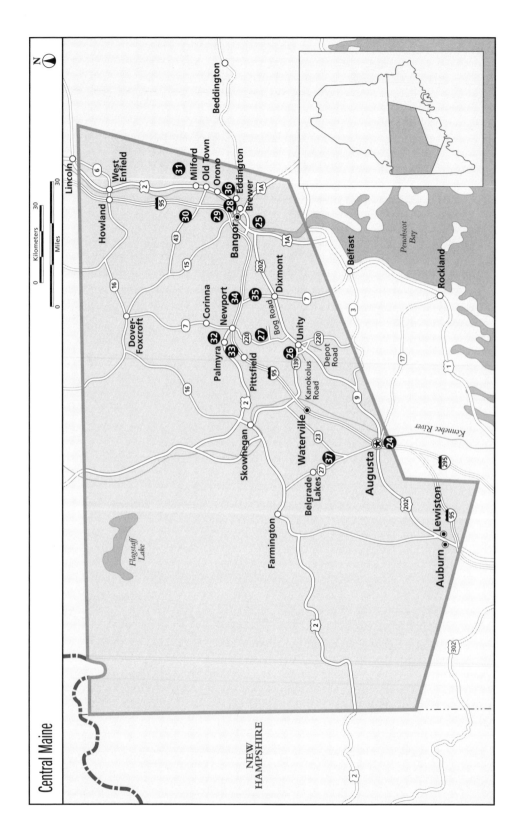

Central Maine

㉔ Pine Tree State Arboretum

Habitats: Wetlands, a small pond, open fields, mixed hardwoods, native shrubs, and botanical gardens.

Best time to bird: Spring and fall songbird migrations are prime times for smaller, land-based birds. Some (American Woodcock, American Robin, Turkey Vulture) arrive as early as late March, and the migration and breeding season continues into May. Summer is productive, too, especially during early morning and late evening.

Nearest gas, food, and lodging: Augusta, Maine's capital city, abounds in inns, motels, and restaurants. Gas is readily available.

Nearest camping: Green Valley Campground, 1248 Cross Hill Road, Vassalboro; (207) 923-3000. Lake St. George State Park, Route 3, Liberty; (207) 589-4255.

For more information: Pine Tree State Arboretum, P.O. Box 344, Augusta, ME 04332-0344; (207) 621-0031; www.pinetreestatearboretum .org; e-mail ptsaso@adelphia.net.

For information on Alonzo Garcelon WMA, contact Maine Department of Inland Fisheries and Wildlife, 284 State Street, 41 State House Station, Augusta, ME 04333-0041; (207) 287-8000; www.mefishwildlife.com.

For the City of Augusta, visit www.ci.augusta .me.us/.

Directions: From the intersection of Routes 9 and 17 in Augusta, drive south for about 0.5 mile. Look for a field and a sign for the arboretum on your left (east) side of the road. *DeLorme: Maine Atlas and Gazetteer:* Page 12, C5

The birds

Around 120 different bird species have been noted at the arboretum. Songbirds, wading birds, waterfowl, grassland birds, and raptors are present. Some key species include Sora and Virginia Rail, Indigo Bunting, Bobolink, and Meadowlark. Eastern Bluebird are occasional visitors.

About this site

Owned by the State of Maine since the mid–1800s, the present site was used as farmland to produce fresh farm products for patients at the Augusta Mental Health Institute. Development of the arboretum commenced in 1981, and in 1982 the Pine Tree State Arboretum, a nonprofit corporation, was formed.

This 224-acre parcel contains about 75 acres of forest land, nearly 150 acres of open fields, and 5 miles of hiking trails. These trails are open daily from sunrise to sunset year-round. Admission is free, but donations are accepted. The Viles Visitor Center is open from 9:00 a.m. to 4:00 p.m. Monday through Friday. Stop in and pick up a brochure and map. The goal of the arboretum is to "promote the knowledge and appreciation of trees, shrubs, and other plants for enjoyment, inspiration, recreation, scientific research, education and aesthetic purposes." In the course of meeting those goals, the arboretum creates and preserves excellent bird habitat.

The Pine Tree State Arboretum features rolling fields, woodlands, and wetlands and is a favorite of local birders.

Nearby opportunities

The Augusta area is rich in birding opportunities. Foremost of these is the Kennebec River, which flows through downtown Augusta. Birds seen on, over, and along the river include Ring-neck Duck, Bald Eagle, Double-crested Cormorant, Great Blue Heron, Common Merganser, Herring Gull, Ringbill Gull, Kingbird, and Osprey.

To reach downtown Augusta on Interstate 95 from points south, take exit 109 and turn right (east) onto Western Avenue. Follow Western Avenue to the downtown area. Here look for benches along the river at any number of obvious locations. This is a great birding spot, especially in winter. December through March are probably the best times to see waterfowl.

The Alonzo Garcelon Wildlife Management Area (WMA) can be scanned from a small roadside turnoff. To fully explore this parcel, you can also launch a canoe and paddle down a small stream that flows through the wetland. A variety of waterfowl make this a popular duck-hunting area in fall, so May and early June, as well as the summer months, would probably be best here for casual birding. To reach the Church Hill Road Parcel (one of four, separate parcels), drive east from Augusta on Route 3, and turn left (north) onto Church Hill Road, about 2 miles out from town. Continue on Church Hill Road for about 3.4 miles, and look for a stream crossing and gravel turnoff on the left (west) side of the road. *DeLorme: Maine Atlas and Gazetteer:* Page 13, B1

25 Fields Pond Audubon Center

Habitats: Mixed-growth forest, meadows, pond, and wetland.

Best time to bird: One of the nicer aspects of Fields Pond Audubon Center is that a good assortment of birds are on hand year-round. The spring warbler migration is a productive time to visit, but a great many other land-based birds spend the summer here. Good viewing does not end with the fall migration. A great variety of birds are in residence in winter, including Bald Eagle, several finches, American Tree Sparrow, a number of woodpeckers, Ruffed Grouse, and Wild Turkey.

Nearest gas, food, and lodging: Brewer, to the north, and Bucksport, to the south, offer plenty of choices for food, lodging, and fuel.

Nearest camping: Masthead Campground, Bucksport; (207) 469-3482.

For more information: Fields Pond Audubon Center, 216 Fields Pond Road, Holden, ME 04429; (207) 989-2591; e-mail fields pond@juno.com.

Directions: From the intersection of U.S. Route 1A and Green Point Road in Brewer (look for a McDonald's restaurant), take Green Point Road south and drive 1 mile to its intersection with Wiswell Road. Turn left (east) onto Wiswell Road, and drive 1.5 miles to Fields Pond Road on the right. Turn right (south) onto Fields Pond Road and drive about 1 mile to the nature center. *DeLorme: Maine Atlas and Gazetteer:* Page 23, C3

The birds

Of the more than 148 species noted at the center, 79 are common here and are likely to be seen (or heard) in season. Among these are Bald Eagle, Osprey, American Bittern, Great Blue Heron, Northern Harrier, Virginia Rail, Spotted Sandpiper, Chimney Swift, Pileated Woodpecker, Marsh Wren, Eastern Bluebird, and Baltimore Oriole. Add to these a number of warblers and waterbirds.

Look for Bobolink and Savannah Sparrow around the fields. Nesting species at the center include American Bittern, Black-backed Woodpecker, and Blue-winged Teal.

About this site

The sanctuary is a gift to the Maine Audubon Society from the late Katherine Curran, bequeathed in 1994. The Curran family operated these 192 acres as a working farm. The gift included 1,600 feet of shoreline property on Fields Pond, fields, woods, wetlands, and a 22-acre island on the pond.

Today, features include walking trails through fields and woodlands and a 300-foot boardwalk through a floodplain swamp. The wheelchair-accessible Nature Center Building is open to the public admission-free. The center contains informative displays and a shop where you can buy such items as binoculars and field guides. The sanctuary features weekly natural history programs, nature walks, and field trips year-round and seasonal day camp programs for children.

Fields Pond and the surrounding fields and woodlands attract birds—and birders—year-round.

Nearby opportunities
The city of Brewer has placed benches alongside the Penobscot River, along Route 15. This riverside park is a good place to view Bald Eagle and a variety of gulls.

26 Unity Pond

Habitats: Wetland, pond, stream, and riparian habitat.

Best time to bird: May and early June are best for walking along the road by the boat landing and looking for warblers. Osprey and Bald Eagle are evident, and you have a good chance to encounter either of both species. At this time you will also hear American Bittern, particularly in the late afternoon. In summer eagles glide over the pond. If you have a boat, head across the pond to Big Island and see the eagle's nest. Migrating waterfowl are here in good numbers beginning in September and lasting through October.

Nearest camping: Sebasticook Lake Campground, Newport; (800) 319-9333. Christie's Campground and Cottages, Newport; (800) 688-5141.

For more information: To learn more about Kanokolus Beach or to purchase a season ticket, call (207) 948-3763. For information on wildlife around Unity Pond, contact Maine Department of Inland Fisheries and Wildlife, 284 State Street, 41 State House Station, Augusta, ME 04333-0041; (207) 287-8000; www.mefishwildlife.com

Directions: On U.S. Route 202 in Unity Village, look for Kanokolus Road, which is diagonally across from Depot Road. Drive northeast on Kanokolus Road. After passing a large cemetery on both sides of the road, slow down and look for vernal pools on both sides of the road. The thick growth around these pools hosts migrating spring warblers. Continue along Kanokolus Road, cross the Belfast and Moosehead Lake Railroad tracks, and park at the lot at the public landing at Unity Pond. *DeLorme: Maine Atlas and Gazetteer:* Page 22, D1

The birds

A prime waterfowl production area. Expect to see shovelers, Ring-necked Duck, American Black Duck, and Wood Duck. Other large birds include Canada Goose, Great Blue Heron, American Bittern, Osprey, and Bald Eagle. Look for an active eagle's nest atop a tall white pine on the north end of Big Island.

Smaller birds include Virginia Rail, Yellow Warbler and Red-winged Blackbird. The high ground between the lake and the wetland is filled with migrating spring warblers.

About this site

Unity Pond is one of those little-known places where locals go birding. Access is easy, thanks to the public boat launching area. A small beach, dock, picnic tables, and parking area make this a popular spot on weekends in summer. From Memorial Day to Labor Day, the town charges a $2 parking fee. This is primarily enforced on weekends, though. Birders mostly come here in spring and spend their time walking along Kanokolus Road, checking the edges for warblers and also scanning the wetlands that bound the pond.

Bald Eagle are nesting at Unity Pond.

Boaters can launch at the ramp, head to the left (north), and follow the shoreline to where Sandy Stream exits the pond. This sluggish stream winds through a large wetland, the same one viewed from Kanokolus Road. By paddling slowly, and hugging one side or the other of the stream, you can get close-up views of Great Blue Heron. The streamside brush hosts lots of Yellow Warbler in spring, and Tree Swallow dart and dive overhead, picking insects out of the air. If you are really lucky, you may get a glimpse of an American Bittern as it cautiously moves about in the yellow marsh grass.

Nearby opportunities

The Sandy Stream Division, a satellite of Sunkhaze National Wildlife Refuge, located at the intersections of Route 139 and Prairie Road in Unity, hosts Sedge Wren, a species on the Maine endangered species list.

㉗ Carlton Pond Waterfowl Production Area

Habitats: 1,055-acre pond, marsh, and wetland.

Best time to bird: From late April through June, waterfowl are much in evidence. In June visitors can see Black Tern flying over the pond. For this reason alone, June rates as the absolute best month to visit. The fall migration, September and October, is another good time. In summer Osprey glide high above the pond.

Nearest gas, food, and lodging: The small store at the intersection of US 202/Route 9 and US 220 in Troy offers a wide variety of take-out foods. Nearby Newport has lots of restaurants and motels.

Nearest camping: Christie's Campground and Cottages, RR 2, Newport; (800) 688-5141. Sebasticook Lake Campground, Newport; (800) 319-9333.

For more information: Carlton Pond Waterfowl Production Area, 1168 Main Street, Old Town, ME 04468; (207) 827-6138; www.sunk haze.org.

For information on St. Albans Wildlife Management Area, contact Maine Department of Inland Fisheries and Wildlife, 284 State Street, 41 State House Station, Augusta, ME 04333-0041; call (207) 287-8000; www.mefishwildlife.com.

Directions: From the intersection of U.S. Route 202/Route 9 and State Route 220 about 2.6 miles west of Troy, drive north on Route 220 for about 3 miles to Bog Road on the right (east) side of the road near a stream crossing. At this corner look for a National Wildlife Refuge sign, featuring the familiar stylized depiction of a goose. Turn right (east) onto Bog Road and drive for about 0.5 mile to a small semicircular dirt parking area on the right. This is the parking area for Carlton Pond Waterfowl Production Area. *DeLorme: Maine Atlas and Gazetteer:* Page 22, C1

The birds

Carlton Pond is a key breeding area for the Maine endangered Black Tern. The area is rich in waterfowl species, as well as American Bittern and Virginia and Sora Rail. Also present are Great Blue Heron. Green-backed Heron are documented here as well. During the migration, besides the standard array of ducks, you may also see Pintail, Wigeon, Shoveler and White-winged Scoter.

About this site

The U.S. Fish and Wildlife Service purchased Carlton Pond Waterfowl Production Area in 1966 to ensure that this valuable habitat would remain open to waterfowl and other wildlife species. In 1972 the present dam (with flood-control capability) replaced the original rock structure, erected in 1850.

In addition to the Maine endangered Black Tern, Slend Blue Flag, a plant on the Maine list of threatened species, grows here. Plant enthusiasts will find an impressive number of peatland plants here.

Birders can enjoy Carlton Pond in two ways. First, park in the small lot off Bog Road and walk across the road to the dam. There you can stand or sit and scan the

Carlton Pond, viewed here from the road, can be birded either from shore or via canoe.

water and bog with binoculars or scope. Second, and better, launch a canoe and explore the pond and edge habitat at your leisure.

Nearby opportunities

Big Meadow Bog, between Pittsfield and Burnham, can be birded from any of a number of points along Horseback Road. Look for Bald Eagle, ospreys, loons, waterfowl, and wading birds. Begin at the bridge over Sebasticook River on the Somerset/Waldo County line. This is also the beginning of the Sebasticook River trip, a popular canoeing adventure, and a popular fishing spot, with black crappie, smallmouth bass, and white perch the key species. You can find plenty of parking on the Pittsfield (north) end of the bridge and also a good, gravel boat-launch site. From here, head south along Horseback Road for 5.7 miles, during which the road passes fields and wetlands and finally crosses Meadow Brook. Here, look for another large roadside turnout. While both sides of the road are private property, this wide, wet meadow can be birded from the road. From here, continue south to Unity or return to Pittsfield.

28 Saxl Park

Habitats: Gravel trails wind about through mowed fields and past hedgerows filled with wild fruit trees, red osier dogwood, highbush cranberry, and hawthorn shrubs. Also here is a small marsh area.

Best time to bird: Saxl Park is blessed with a good variety of interesting birds year-round. It's hard to say what season is best here. The springtime migration, which warms up here in May, has its share of birds. The grassland birds of summer are a draw, too. Fall and winter continue to present birds of interest. Essentially, you can expect rewarding birding any time you visit Saxl Park.

Nearest gas, food, and lodging: Bangor, the largest city in Central Maine, is filled with restaurants, motels and inns, and gas stations.

Nearest camping: Paul Bunyan Campground, Bangor; (207) 941-1177. Pleasant Hill RV Park and Campground, Bangor; (207) 848-5127.

For more information: Call (207) 941-4023. The Fred Boyce Trail, which winds through most of the park, is listed on the Healthy Maine Walks Web site: www.healthymaine walks.org.

Directions: From downtown Bangor head northeast on U.S. Route 2 (State Street), and look on the right for the large complex of buildings that make up Eastern Maine Medical Center. From here continue only 0.4 mile to a sign for Bangor Mental Health Institute on the left (north) side of road, just past Cascade Park. Turn left and drive 0.3 mile to a stop sign. Turn left at this T inter-section and look for the Maine Department of Inland Fisheries and Wildlife building (marked by a conspicuous sign) on the immediate left. You can park behind this building. Or you may simply wish to park at Cascade Park and follow a trail along the stream (an artificial cascade). This trail takes you into Saxl Park. *DeLorme: Maine Atlas and Gazetteer:* Page 23, B2

The birds

Grassland birds here include Savannah Sparrow, Bobolink, and Meadowlark. Also common are Brown Thrasher, Tree Swallow, Yellow Warbler, Pine Grosbeak, Ameri-can Redstart, American Crow, and American Robin. Also seen fairly regularly are Merlin, Peregrine Falcon, American Kestrel and, in fall and spring, Northern Harrier.

Look for Red-winged Blackbird in spring and summer, especially around the cattail-filled marshy area. In winter Bohemian Waxwing flock here for berries cling-ing to bushes. Another occasional winter visitor, the Northern Shrike, sometimes leaves evidence of its presence by impaling small rodents on hawthorn thorns.

Saxl Park, being an open area close to the Penobscot River, has its share of gulls, too. Besides the ubiquitous Herring Gull, Saxl Park hosts a smorgasbord of other gulls, including Ring-billed, Great Black-backed, Iceland, and Glaucous Gull.

About this site

Saxl Park, 100 acres of field and shrub on the grounds of the Bangor Mental Health Institute (BMHI), is an oasis of green (brown in fall and early spring) in the

Saxl Park is an island of nature on the edge of downtown Bangor.

midst of one of central Maine's largest urban areas. Located so close to a commercial center, the park is a favorite haunt of local workers on their lunch break, as well as others who frequent the fields for impromptu picnics. Joggers and walkers use the approximately 3 miles of gravel walking trails. Birders, except for the scant handful who are aware of this excellent site, are in the minority.

The park is named for Joseph Saxl, BMHI Superintendent from 1976 to 1981. Saxl had a vision of sharing the park with the community, and the present status of the park is due to his efforts.

Nearby opportunities

Saxl Park borders Cascade Park, a popular site on weekends for Bangor residents. Cascade Park offers ample parking, and before heading for Saxl Park, visitors can walk across US 2 and scan the Penobscot River above the crumbling Bangor Dam. Bald Eagle ply the river here; Barrow's Goldeneye sometimes visit in winter. The same species of gulls present at Saxl Park can be expected to be visible on the river.

29 Orono Bog Boardwalk

Habitats: Mixed wooded fen, conifer wooded fen, moss lawn, and wooded shrub heath.

Best time to bird: Beginning in mid-May, birders enjoy the warbler migration. Nesting waterfowl are also in evidence at this time. May and June are excellent times to hear, if not see, the thunderous, pumping call of American Bittern. Through the summer, land-based birds are active during early-morning and evening hours. The boardwalk is open from May 1 through Thanksgiving and may close sooner in the event of early snows.

Access: The Orono Bog Boardwalk is wheelchair accessible. Little physical activity is required, and there are no significant grades.

Nearest gas, food, and lodging: Motels, restaurants, malls, and shops abound in nearby Bangor and Orono. Gas is readily available.

Nearest camping: Paul Bunyan Campground, Bangor; (207) 941-1177. Pleasant Hill RV Park and Campground, Bangor; (207) 848-5127.

For more information: Contact John Daigle, boardwalk director, (207) 581-2850; e-mail john.daigle@umit.maine.edu.

Directions: From Bangor drive north on Interstate 95 to exit 193 in Orono. From there, take a left and drive south on Stillwater Avenue for 4.7 miles to Tripp Road, on the right (west) side of the road. Follow Tripp Road for 0.3 mile to the parking area and trailhead. *DeLorme: Maine Atlas and Gazetteer:* Page 23, A3

The birds

The birding potential for the Orono Bog Boardwalk may not yet be fully realized. The site is relatively new, and birders are just now discovering it. Compiling the list of birds seen from the boardwalk is an ongoing task.

Of particular interest, though, are the migrating spring warblers. The bog hosts a great number of warblers—17 different warblers have been noted thus far. A warbler-watching trip here in May, with spring peepers and wood frogs serenading the birder, is highly recommended.

Birds you would expect to see around wetlands and ponds are here, too, including Common Loon, Double-crested Cormorant, American Bittern, Kildeer, Common Snipe, Canada Goose, and a number of ducks.

Also common are flycatchers, vireos, wrens, and kinglets. Woodpeckers noted here include Yellow-bellied Sapsucker; Downy, Hairy, Pileated Woodpecker; and Northern Flicker. Black-backed Woodpecker have yet to be reported, but it is probably only a matter of time before somebody sees one. If you are that person, or if you see any other bird of special interest, please contact Judy Markowsky at jkm@trefoil.com.

About this site

The Orono Bog Boardwalk takes birders through a series of habitats that would not otherwise be possible to traverse on foot. Besides the birds, Orono Bog is

The 1-mile-long Orono Bog Boardwalk is completely wheelchair accessible.

home to many different plants, insects, amphibians, and mammals. It is truly a nature lover's dream. Besides being wheelchair accessible, the 1-mile boardwalk features benches, placed every 200 feet of its length. Full-color interpretative signs along the boardwalk present information on the plants and wildlife found in and around the bog.

Guided tours of the boardwalk may be arranged for groups. Send an e-mail to wendalltre@aol.com for details.

The boardwalk is part of the larger Bangor Forest—a 650-acre working forest with 9.2 miles of walking and cross-country ski trails. Leashed dogs are permitted on trails; they are not permitted on the boardwalk. Pick up a map of the Bangor Forest at the trailhead at the end of Tripp Road.

Since the Orono Bog is a type of wetland, expect lots of mosquitoes in summer and blackflies in spring. Blackflies are most oppressive in May and June. Given the presence of the West Nile virus, visitors are urged to protect themselves from biting insects. The most efficient way to do this is to apply a DEET-based insect repellent. Whatever kind of insect repellent you choose, make sure to coat all exposed skin.

Nearby opportunities

Orono Bog is owned in part by the University of Maine in Orono. Visit the university's flower and shrub garden (look for warblers here in May) for a pleasant diversion. The university hosts a farm and home museum, a performing arts center, a museum of anthropology, a museum of art, and a planetarium. For more on this campus, contact University of Maine, Orono, ME 04469; (207) 581-1110; www.umaine.edu.

Kenduskeag Stream Park, a birding destination within the Bangor city limits, offers a scenic walk and plenty of birding opportunities for such species as Belted Kingfisher, Double-crested Cormorant, Common Merganser, Common Yellow-throat, Northern Waterthrush, and Bald Eagle. Numerous familiar land birds inhabit the riparian habitat along the stream. To reach the park, from the corner of State and Harlow Streets in Bangor, drive 0.7 mile west on Harlow Street to a parking area. Look for a sign for Kenduskeag Stream Park.

30 Hirundo Wildlife Refuge

Habitats: Fields, stream, spruce-fir forest, and pond; wildlife plantings around field edges and near refuge headquarters.

Best time to bird: May is a top month because of returning swallows and waterfowl and the warbler migration. An interesting way to bird here in late April and May is by canoe. Pushaw Stream overflows its banks, and you can cover much of Hirundo Wildlife Refuge without leaving your canoe. In summer, beginning in June, songbirds are best viewed early and late in the day. However, the feeding station behind the refuge managers' house draws birds year-round. This is a prime spot for getting a close-up photo of any number of songbirds.

Access: While not wheelchair accessible, persons with limited mobility will find the area around the managers' residence—particularly the elaborate bird-feeding station—easy to reach. Trails are regularly cleared and, except for times of high water, present no great physical challenge.

Nearest gas, food, and lodging: Full services are available in nearby Old Town.

Nearest camping: Pushaw Lake Campground, Orono; (207) 945-4200.

For more information: Call (207) 394-4681 or e-mail hirundo@midspring.com. See *Maine Off the Beaten Path* (The Globe Pequot Press, 2006) for further information on places to go in Old Town.

Directions: From Interstate 95 in Old Town, take exit 197 to Route 43. Drive west on Route 43 for 4.5 miles, and look for sanctuary signs on the right-hand side of the road. *DeLorme: Maine Atlas and Gazetteer:* Page 33, E2

The birds

Pushaw Stream and the four-acre pond attract a variety of ducks. Species noted here include Mallard, American Black Duck, Pintail, American Widgeon, Green-winged Teal, Blue-winged Teal, Wood Duck, Common Goldeneye, Common Merganser, Hooded Merganser, and Red-breasted Merganser. Additionally, Pie-billed Grebe have been spotted.

Hawks common to Hirundo include Sharp-shinned, Northern Harrier, and Broad-winged Hawk.

Hirundo hosts Great Blue Heron and American Bittern. Shorebirds include Killdeer, Spotted Sandpiper, and Common Snipe. American Woodcock are common as well.

Migrating spring warblers stop at Hirundo. Most common woodpeckers are present, including Pileated Woodpecker. Several varieties of swallows spend spring and summer here, and Gray Jay are occasionally sighted.

About this site

Founded as a private trust by Oliver Larouche in 1976, Hirundo Wildlife Refuge was donated to the University of Maine in 1983 to be used for educational

This sign marks the entrance to Hirundo Wildlife Refuge, listed on the National Register of Historic Places.

purposes. The refuge is now a self-supporting trust, administered by the Trustees of Hirundo Wildlife Refuge. Funding comes from private donations, not from the university.

This 2,605-acre refuge has color-coded trails leading through forests, along field edges, and around the pond. A total of 125 Tree Swallow houses, placed along the field edges, are a scene of hectic activity in early spring. The 110 Wood Duck nesting boxes are spread in both wetland and upland areas. A walk here on a May or early-June afternoon will disclose Blue Heron, bitterns, and a variety of ducks.

Visitors come here not only to bird but also to hike the trails and to view wildlife. Upland species found on the refuge include white-tailed deer, red fox, fisher, pine marten, flying squirrel, bobcat, raccoon, and porcupine. Wildlife found along Pushaw Stream includes moose, mink, river otter, muskrat, and beaver.

While trails are well maintained, those near Pushaw Stream are often impassable in early spring and during other times of high water. It is then that birders visit Hirundo by canoe. In winter Hirundo's trails serve as cross-country ski trails. If you come here in winter, don't attempt to walk on the ice on Pushaw Stream—it is never fully safe.

Hirundo Wildlife Refuge is listed on the National Register of Historic Places. As the refuge was being developed, artifacts from the long-vanished Red Paint People were found along the stream. Accordingly, the site became a "dig," and professors and students from University of Maine unearthed and catalogued the artifacts.

Guests are asked to register and pick up a trail map at the gate.

Nearby opportunities

Caribou Bog Wetland Complex, one of the largest of its kind in Maine, covers about 6,000 acres. An assortment of rare and unusual plants is found here, as well as some uncommon wading birds and marsh birds. An easy way to see at least part of this is to take the Caribou Bog hike, described in *Hiking Maine,* Globe Pequot Press, 2002. To reach the trailhead, drive about 6 miles north from Bangor on Stillwater Avenue and turn left (west) onto Forest Avenue in Orono. Drive 1.5 miles. Look for a road to the right, with a small parking area. This is the entrance to the Orono Landfill, so be sure not to block the road. You will see signs for trucks entering. You can also pull off the road on the left, since the trailhead is on the left. Look for the trailhead on MAG, Map 23, A3.

While in the area, a trip to the Penobscot River may prove worthwhile. Birders can scan the river for ducks and geese throughout the season, except when it is frozen. A walking path in downtown Old Town offers birding possibilities, and you can also cross the river here and head either south on Route 178 or north on U.S. Route 2. Both ways offer numerous places to park and to get out and walk around. Look for Bald Eagle and a variety of ducks.

31 Sunkhaze Meadows National Wildlife Refuge

Habitats: Streams, wetlands, forested uplands of hardwood; spruce-fir forest, a peat bog (for which the refuge is named), and pioneer growth on edge of trail.

Best time to bird: Try to hit the late-spring migration. This lasts from June through early July and is the absolute best time to visit Sunkhaze Meadows. September and October are also good months for waterfowl viewing.

Nearest gas, food, and lodging: Old Town has plenty of restaurants; Bangor and Orono are filled with motels and inns, restaurants, and gas stations.

Nearest camping: Pushaw Lake Campground, Orono; (207) 945-4200. Paul Bunyan Campground, Bangor; (207) 941-1177.

For more information: Sunkhaze Meadows National Wildlife Refuge, 1033 South Main Street, Old Town, ME 04468; (207) 827-6138; www.sunkhaze.org. Or contact Friends of Sunkhaze Meadows National Wildlife Refuge, 1168 Main Street, Old Town, ME 04468.

Directions: From U.S. Route 2 in Milford, turn right (east) onto County Road. Drive for 4.2 miles and look for a sign on the left (north) marking Baker Brook. You can put a canoe in here. For Oak Point Trail continue on County Road for another 2.2 miles (a total of 6.4 miles) to a sign for Oak Point Trail, again on the left. This is the trailhead for Oak Point Trail. Park here, but do not block the trailhead entrance. *DeLorme: Maine Atlas and Gazetteer:* Page 33, E4 and E5

The birds

Over 200 species of birds have thus far been documented at Sunkhaze Meadows, and this list continues to grow. It's tempting to say that waterfowl are the key species here. But a wide variety of other types of birds are also present in great numbers. A great array of neotropical migratory songbirds nest at Sunkhaze, including Chestnut-sided Warbler, Scarlet Tanager, and Olive-sided Flycatcher. Also present here are Bobolink and Rose-breasted Grosbeak. Two notable species seen at Sunkhaze are Yellow Rail and Sedge Wren.

For starters, though, expect to see American Black Duck, Wood Duck, Hooded Merganser, Mallard, Ring-necked Duck, and Blue-winged Teal. A list of the larger waterbirds here include Great Blue Heron, American Bittern, and Double-crested Cormorant. Smaller birds of the wetland areas include Virginia and Sora Rail, Spotted Sandpiper, Greater Yellowlegs, Common Snipe, and Long-billed Dowitcher.

Osprey, Northern Harrier, and Broad-winged Hawk are common, as are Barred Owl, Chimney Swift, and Belted Kingfisher. Of the 24 species of warblers noted here, 12 are common springtime arrivals.

These are only some of what you can expect to encounter here. Before visiting Sunkhaze Meadows, it is recommended that you acquire the U.S. Fish & Wildlife Service pamphlet detailing all the birds of Sunkhaze Meadows National Wildlife Refuge.

Birders have noted more than 200 bird species at Sunkhaze Meadows National Wildlife Refuge.

About this site

A relatively new national wildlife refuge, Sunkhaze Meadows was established in 1988, spurred on by a proposed commercial peat extraction effort in the bog. Today the refuge encompasses more than 10,000 acres surrounding about 5 miles of Sunkhaze Stream. The peatland, now secure against exploitation, is one of the largest in Maine.

Birding here is done by walking the hiking trails and canoeing. Oak Point Trail is highly recommended. This 1-mile trail is bounded on three sides by streams and on the fourth side by a road. The end of the trail overlooks the vast expanse of Sunkhaze Meadows. Or you can put your canoe in at Baker Brook and paddle through the wetlands there. Go slowly, and watch carefully.

Sunkhaze Meadows is managed as a "Wildlife First" place and is perfectly wild. There are no facilities of any kind here. With that in mind, take pains to leave no footprint.

Nearby opportunities

Milford is a river town on the Penobscot River. From Milford drive north on US 2 and stop an any of the numerous State of Maine boat launch areas. Here you will see various types of waterfowl. Bald Eagle are common residents on the Penobscot, so keep an eye peeled for the telltale white head of the adult eagle.

32 St. Albans Wildlife Management Area

Habitats: Freshwater marsh and pond; aquatic vegetation includes extensive stands of wild rice. Somewhat limited riparian habitat includes stands of mature white pine, spruce-fir mixed growth, and understory shrubs.

Best time to bird: Beginning in mid-May and continuing through June, breeding water-fowl keep the marsh alive with activity. Summer is relatively quiet, but the fall migration in September and October bring the marsh back to life.

Access: Two-wheel-drive vehicles can easily reach the impounded wetland. Walking is pos-sible around much of the wetland, and various opportunities exist to launch a canoe.

Nearest food and lodging: Nearby Newport has motels and plenty of restaurants and take-out food services. Find gas in Corinna.

Nearest camping: Christie's Campground and Cottages, Newport; (207) 368-4645 or (800) 688-5141 (reservations).

For more Information: Contact Maine Department of Inland Fisheries and Wildlife, Sidney Regional Office, at (207) 547-5300 or the department's main office in Augusta at (207) 287-8000.

Directions: From Route 7 in Corinna, turn left (south) onto Nokomis Road. This begins by the Corinna Town Library, a large redbrick building with a prominent bell tower. Follow Nokomis Road south for 2.7 miles to the stop sign and intersection with Williams Road. Turn right (north) and drive about 1 mile to a sharp corner. Look for a dirt road on the left (west) side of this corner. Although rains may fill potholes and puddles, making the road look questionable, it has a good, hard surface. Just go slowly, drive in a short distance to the end of the pond, and park by the out-let. From here you can walk about, up and down the south side of the wetland. Also, you can launch a canoe here. *DeLorme: Maine Atlas and Gazetteer:* Page 22, A1

The birds

Waterbirds predominate here. Ducks include Wood Duck, Blue-winged Teal, Hooded Merganser, Ring-necked Duck, Common Goldeneye, Mallard, and Black Duck. Some interesting species observed here in the past include Marsh Wren, American Coot, Common Moorhen, Least Bittern, Green-backed Heron, Spotted Sandpiper, Sora Rail, and Virginia Rail. More likely, though, are American Bittern, Great Blue Heron, Red-winged Blackbird, Osprey, Canada Goose, and Common Grackle. Forest birds frequent the upland habitat.

About this site

St. Albans Wildlife Management Area (WMA) is a hidden gem, not advertised and basically unknown except to a few local birders. Those making the effort to visit will find many rewards. Except for October and November hunting seasons, and this mostly on Saturday (Sunday hunting is prohibited in Maine), the WMA is bereft of human presence.

The riparian habitat at St. Albans WMA may yield American Bittern, Great Blue Heron, Red-winged Blackbird, Osprey, Canada Goose, and Common Grackle.

Birding is easily accomplished from shore with either binoculars or a scope. Excellent views across the marsh can be had from the earthen dam near the entrance road. A canoe provides access to the more distant and remote sections of the marsh. Try paddling along the marsh edges to break up your outline. Go slowly, and stop to look and listen every so often.

Nearby opportunities

Sprague's Mill, a small roadside park about 0.5 mile south of downtown Corinna on Route 222, sits along a small, shallow pond. Ducks and other waterfowl frequent the pond, and some songbirds are present around the upland area below the dam. Picnic tables here offer a place to sit and scan the pond and marshy edges with binoculars.

33 Madawaska Wildlife Management Area

Habitats: Large, partially flooded sedge meadow; open-water areas and stands of wild rice.

Best time to bird: A visit here any time from mid-May through June will be most productive for breeding marshbirds and waterfowl. Migrating waterfowl bring the marsh alive again in fall, from late September and lasting until November.

Access: While some birding at Madawaska WMA is possible from the parking area, a canoe is definitely an asset here. The wetland along Douglas Pond can be birded by foot.

Nearest gas, food, and lodging: Fuel and lodging are available in Palmyra and Newport. Both towns have a good number of restaurants and take-out food services.

Nearest camping: Christie's Campground and Cottages, Newport; (800) 688-5141.

For more information: Contact Maine Department of Inland Fisheries and Wildlife, Sidney Regional Office, at (207) 547-5300 or the department's main office in Augusta at (207) 287-8000.

Directions: From Newport head west on U.S. Route 2 to Palmyra. About 2 miles past the town center, turn left (south) onto Madawaska Road, and drive 1.2 miles to a sign for the WMA and a spacious parking area on the left (east) side of the road. *DeLorme: Maine Atlas and Gazetteer:* Page 21, B5

The birds

Madawaska Wildlife Management Area (WMA) has a small but good marshbird diversity. Viewing the state-endangered Black Tern is possible here, since they nest at nearby Douglas Pond. Ducks here include Black and Wood Duck, Blue-winged Teal, Hooded Merganser, and Common Merganser. Also present are Canada Goose, Great Blue Heron, American Bittern, Virginia Rail, Sora Rail, Common Snipe, and Spotted Sandpiper. Marsh Wren have been observed here, as have Pied-billed Grebe. Other birds noted include Northern Harrier, Belted Kingfisher, Red-winged Blackbird, and Common Grackle.

About this site

Easy access highlights Madawaska WMA. This includes plenty of roadside parking and an easy launch site for canoes. While some birding is possible from the parking area, a canoe enables the birder to wring the fullest amount of enjoyment from the area.

Madawaska WMA is part of a larger wetland complex that encompasses Douglas Pond and surrounding wetlands. Consequently, these two geographic areas often share birds. Madawaska WMA, while relatively small, is typical of many larger, better-known waterbird sites and shares many of their characteristics. As with so many of the other WMAs listed in this book, Madawaska is an ideal destination for birders seeking seclusion, tranquility, and, most of all, lots of desirable bird species to view.

Birders might glimpse the state-endangered Black Tern at the Madawaska WMA.

Nearby opportunities

Douglas Pond is connected to Madawaska WMA by Madawaska Brook. There is a nesting Black Tern colony here. Birders can gain foot access to Douglas Pond via the Pittsfield-Hartland Multiuse Trail running along the western side of the pond, beginning at US 2 in West Palmyra and continuing south to Route 152 in Pittsfield. Take this trail in spring for migrating warblers. Douglas Pond contains black crappie, white perch, and largemouth bass, making it a favorite destination for anglers.

34 Durham Bridge

Habitats: Open water on lake, freshwater marsh, mudflats.

Best time to bird: Beginning in late March (provided that subfreezing weather doesn't linger), waterfowl return to Sebasticook Lake, and Durham Bridge is a good place to watch the show. Kingfishers begin their visit in May and stay throughout the summer. Duck activity slows down in July and August, picks up again in September, and continues through November. Exposed mudflats in late summer attract shorebirds in good numbers. Low water, and good shorebird viewing, often lasts through October.

Access: Foot access to the causeway and canoe access to the lake are both available.

Nearest gas, food, and lodging: Newport has stores, restaurants, and lodging of all types. Fuel is available in Newport and East Newport.

Nearest camping: Christie's Campground and Cottages, Newport; (207) 368-4645 or (800) 688-5141 (reservations); Sebasticook Lake Campground, Newport; (800) 688-5141.

For more information: While roadside birding does not typically fall under their jurisdiction, the Maine Department of Inland Fisheries and Wildlife can probably give you an idea of what conditions to expect at any particular time of year. Call the Region B office in Sidney at (287) 547-5300 or the department's head office in Augusta at (207) 287-8000.

Directions: From the intersection of Stetson Road and Route 7 and U.S. Route 2 in East Newport, head north on Stetson Road. Drive for 2.4 miles on Stetson Road to a four-way intersection with Durham Bridge Road. Turn left (northwest) on Durham Bridge Road, and drive another 1.7 miles to the bridge and causeway. *DeLorme: Maine Atlas and Gazetteer:* Page 22, A1

The birds

Durham Bridge is part of a causeway spanning a narrow finger of Sebasticook Lake. Ducks and shorebirds are key here, but other interesting birds include Common Loon, Canada Goose, and Belted Kingfisher. American Bittern and Virginia Rail sometimes frequent the marshy section to the east side of the causeway. Shorebirds here include both Greater and Lesser Yellowlegs, Semipalmated Sandpiper, Least Sandpiper, and Common Snipe.

Expect to see Mallard, Hooded Merganser, Common Merganser, and Green-winged Teal. Beginning in May and lasting all summer, you will probably see Belted Kingfisher sitting on utility lines along the causeway. Spot a kingfisher and watch closely. Eventually the bird will rocket from the wires, emit a loud chatter, and slam into the water for a fish. With luck, you might get to see the bird successfully catch a minnow or small spiny-rayed fish.

It is probably safe to say that more people visit here for shorebirds than ducks. Late summer (August) often brings low water levels, exposing mudflats. This rich mud attracts shorebirds through October.

In fall the water level here at Durham Bridge drops precipitously.

About this site

Durham Bridge and attached causeway provide foot access to Sebasticook Lake, a productive waterfowl site. While birding can be done from either side of the causeway, it's probably not a good idea to stand on the bridge itself. The bridge is slightly narrower than the causeway, leaving scant room for both pedestrians and motor vehicles. Riprap (stones) on either side of the bridge, though, provides good places to sit and watch.

Two boat launch sites, here at the north end of the causeway, accommodate both trailerable and hand-carry watercraft. On the east side of the road, the hand-carry site allows for launching canoes and car-top boats. The launch on the west side, on the larger part of the lake, allows for launching boats on trailers. A small parking area accommodates three or four vehicles.

In spring, birders share the causeway with anglers from near and far. White perch make their annual spawning runs here in May, and thousands of these silvery cousins of the striped bass cross under Durham Bridge on their way to and from their spawning grounds. Common Loon and other fish-eating waterbirds follow the runs, making this a great time for a close look at a loon. People, too, line the causeway each evening during the run. Birds here have adapted well to this human activity; ducks, geese, and even Common Loon will occasionally swim past within feet of the causeway.

During high-water years, a dam on the opposite side of the lake is opened to release great volumes of water. This is a precautionary measure, meant to bring water levels down to accommodate winter snow and ice and, in turn, prevent springtime flooding.

If ever there were a family-oriented birding site, this is it. Bring some folding chairs, a few fishing rods for the kids, and a set of binoculars for adult birders, and you have the ingredients for many pleasure-filled hours.

For those coming in late summer and fall to watch the shorebirds, a spotting scope will serve you well. Walking on the mudflats is possible but not advisable. It's better to set up your scope on hard, dry land and scan the area that way.

Nearby opportunities

The bridge over Alder Stream on County Road, on the north end of Sebasticook Lake, offers good waterfowl viewing. Recent road construction has done away with what little parking was available around the bridge, making it necessary for birders and others to park just off the road, away from the bridge. That said, the slow-moving stream and marsh hold lots of waterfowl. Remember those binoculars.

(35) Plymouth Pond

Habitats: 780-acre pond spanned by a causeway; sedge-meadow wetland.

Best time to bird: Black Tern nest here from May to August, with most likely sightings in late-May or June. Waterfowl begin showing up as soon as ice begins to melt in spring, which often is in mid-March. A culvert along the causeway that bisects the pond constricts the flow, causing a current. Here water freezes late and melts early.

A visit in late September or October will reward the birder with sightings of various ducks. If you are lucky, you may also encounter migrating snipe and possibly Virginia Rail.

Access: Excellent foot access is available by parking near the boat landing. It is easy to launch a canoe here to explore either or both sides of the pond surrounding wetlands.

Nearest gas, food, and lodging: A general store in Plymouth, near the pond, sells gas, food, and supplies. For restaurants, motels, and inns, head for nearby Pittsfield or Newport.

Nearest camping: Christie's Campground and Cottages, Newport; (207) 368-4645 or (800) 688-5141 (reservations); Sebasticook Lake Campground, Newport; (800) 688-5141.

For more information: Although private land surrounds Plymouth Pond, Maine's Great Pond Act puts the surface of any 10-acre or larger naturally occurring pond under public domain. If you're near the shore, though, respect private landowners' property rights.

Directions: From the intersection of Route 7 and U.S. Route 202/Route 9 in Dixmont, drive north on Route 7. Travel for 6.3 miles to the causeway and gravel boat landing and parking area on the left. *DeLorme: Maine Atlas and Gazetteer:* Page 22, B2

The birds

Plymouth Pond is an excellent waterfowl site as well as a place to view marshbirds. The latter include American Bittern, Virginia Rail, Wilson's Snipe, and Black Tern. Marsh Wren, another desirable addition to any birder's life list, are found here. Other birds include Red-winged Blackbird, Belted Kingfisher, Northern Harrier, Pied-billed Grebe, Common Loon, and Great Blue Heron. Other wading birds are always possible, as are Osprey.

About this site

Plymouth Pond incorporates many of the attributes necessary for a successful birding trip, including easy access, a long viewing season, and plenty of interesting birds. The 0.7-mile-long causeway allows for a leisurely walk along the pond on one side and a sedge meadow on the other. A public boat launch on a gravel bar and a parking area midway along the causeway (east side) allow for easy launching of a canoe. The culvert is large enough to allow most watercraft to pass through.

As with so many water-based birding sites, a canoe is your ticket to the site's inner reaches. A canoe trip through the wetlands here will up the odds of close encounters with many different bird species. (**Caution:** Black Tern do not tolerate

The 0.7-mile-long causeway crosses Plymouth Pond.

encroachment on their nesting sites. If you see terns flying about, do not get any closer. Instead use your binoculars to better view them. If disturbed, Black Tern may abandon their nests—a death sentence for the young.)

Plymouth Pond rates high as yet another prime site for families to visit. An excellent largemouth bass pond (trophy bass live here), Plymouth also contains pickerel, yellow perch, and white perch. There's ample room at the boat landing for a group to set up folding chairs and watch the pond for birds while others try their luck on bass.

NOTE: Poison ivy grows along the road on both sides of the causeway south of the boat landing. Even in the off-season when leaves are gone, the vines can cause a serious rash. Wear long pants, and don't touch any suspicious roadside vegetation. If you do, wash your hands as soon as possible in fresh water.

Nearby opportunities

A trip down Flood Road, just south of Plymouth Pond, takes you near a large wetland.

36 Leonard's Mills

Habitats: Young growth of alder and other pioneer species; softwood monocultures; mature forest of mixed growth, including white pine and red oak; open ground along power lines; marshland and open water.

Best time to bird: May and June are best for migrating warblers. Marshbirds and waterfowl are active around Blackman Stream. Osprey are on their nests, and with optical aids, the young should be visible high atop the utility poles.

A walk through the mature woods around the mill in summer should yield sightings of a number of forest birds. In September the fall warbler migration will usher in more warblers, and in October and November ducks and perhaps Canada Goose will be evident on Blackman Stream.

Access: Access here is easy, either by foot or by motor vehicle.

Nearest gas, food, and lodging: Gas can be found in Eddingtom and Milford. Brewer and Bangor are major cities and have all the amenities, including restaurants, grocery stores, inns, motels and bed-and-breakfasts.

Nearest camping: Paul Bunyan Campground, Bangor; (207) 941-1177. Pleasant Hill RV Park and Campground, Bangor; (207) 848-5127.

For more information: Call (207) 581-2871 or visit www.leonardsmills.com.

Directions: From the intersection of Routes 9 and 178 in Eddington, drive north on Route 178 for 4.3 miles to a sign for Leonard's Mills on the right (east) side of the road. You can either park near this sign or drive 1 mile to a fork in the gravel road. Turn right here and travel to the parking area for Leonard's Mills. To reach the hiking trails, walk downhill from the parking lot, cross the covered bridge, and look for the trailhead sign by the blacksmith shop. *DeLorme: Maine Atlas and Gazetteer:* Page 23, B3

The birds

Leonard's Mills and vicinity host a great assortment of birds. Warblers draw birders here during spring migration to view Pine, Chestnut-sided, and Black-throated Blue Warbler, to name just a few. Wet areas sometimes host Northern Waterthrush. Other birds include thrushes, Eastern Wood Peewee, Osprey, Double-crested Cormorant, and Great Blue Heron, and Canada Goose. Ruffed Grouse live here, as well as the occasional Spruce Grouse.

About this site

Leonard's Mills is a restored eighteenth-century logging community set along Blackman Stream. Saturdays in summer are busy with different events, but weekdays and Sundays often see the place deserted. The road to Leonard's Mills, through the University of Maine's Penobscot Experimental Forest, crosses a wide variety of habitats, including softwood monocultures. A series of hiking trails, with a trailhead near the actual old mill, takes birders through upland habitat as well as past a freshwater marsh along Blackman Stream.

The covered bridge over Blackman Stream, Leonard's Mills, enhances the scenery.

Lots of people choose to park along the main road near the sign for Leonard's Mills and walk in through the Experimental Forest. This is a popular birding method in spring, when warblers flock to the different habitats.

Where the road (called Government Road on maps) passes under a series of high-tension power lines, look for Osprey nests atop the tall poles.

It would be easy to spend an entire day birding this area, especially if you walk in from the main road, spend time along Blackman Stream at Leonard's Mills, and also walk the hiking trails. A few caveats are in order here. In spring, blackflies—fierce biting gnats—are present in force. Some people wear insect netting; others content themselves with insect repellent. Either way, know that the warbler migration coincides with the height of blackfly season.

Nearby opportunities

Several sites along the Penobscot River between the city of Brewer and Leonard's Mills offer a chance to see Bald Eagle as well as several species of ducks that spend the winter on open-water sections of the river. Within the city of Brewer, Indian Trail Park, on the west side of Routes 178/9, offers ample parking, trails along wooded hills along the river, and some striking river views. Some of the trails go through rugged and steep terrain; extreme caution is needed to get to where you have a good view of the river. Binoculars are a definite help here. *DeLorme: Maine Atlas and Gazetteer:* Page 23, B3

Slightly north of Indian Trail Park, also on the west side of Routes 178/9, is the city of Brewer's river access. Here are picnic tables, parking, and a boat launch site. This is a good place to stop and scan the river when visiting or leaving Leonard's Mills.

37 Belgrade Bog

Habitats: Floating bog mat, sedge meadow, slow-moving stream, lake edge.

Best time to bird: This rates as a prime early-season birding site. If spring comes early, perhaps mid-March or earlier, you may find Canada Goose as well as a number of duck species returning now. Many of these are headed elsewhere and won't stay, but the open water provides them with a good place to rest and refresh themselves before moving on.

Sometime around the second week of May, breeding waterfowl are present in numbers. Marshbirds and others are active, and the bog comes alive with birdsong. In June activity becomes even more intense, making this probably the very best time to visit. Fall, especially late September and the month of October, sees large blocks of migrating ducks and Canada Goose. Bald Eagle cruise the lake in winter, seeking fish left on the ice by anglers.

Access: Foot access along the boat launch at Belgrade Bog is easy and comfortable, as is launching a canoe.

Nearest gas, food, and lodging: Belgrade Lakes has plenty of restaurants and variety stores and several places to buy gas. The Belgrade region is a tourist center and abounds in lodges and bed-and-breakfast establishments. Nearby Augusta also has plenty of choices for food and lodging.

Nearest camping: Two Rivers Campground, Skowhegan; (207) 474-6482. Skowhegan-Canaan KOA Campground, Canaan; (207) 474-2858.

For more information: Maine Department of Inland Fisheries and Wildlife maintains public boat launch sites. The site listed here is closed to trailerable boats. For more information call (207) 287-8000.

Directions: From Augusta head north on Route 27 for about 6 miles, and turn left (west) at the intersection of Routes 27 and 23. Continue north on Route 27 for 3.5 miles to the public boat landing on Belgrade Stream. (To visit Peninsula Park, continue north on Route 27 for another 7 miles to Belgrade Lakes.) Look for the hand-carry public boat landing on the west side of Messalonskee Lake. *DeLorme: Maine Atlas and Gazetteer:* Page 12, A5

The birds

Belgrade Bog on Messalonskee Lake may possibly have the greatest marshbird diversity in Maine. Of special note, the Black Tern colony here is considered one of Maine's largest.

Black Tern are the big draw, but by no means are they the only species of interest. Also recorded here are Pied-billed Grebe, Common Loon, a wide variety of ducks, Double-crested Cormorant, Great Black-backed Gull, American Coot, American Bittern, Least Bittern, Great Blue Heron, Virginia Rail, Common Snipe, Spotted Sandpiper, Marsh Wren, and Common Moorhen.

Eastern Kingbird are regular summertime residents along Belgrade Stream and are easily viewed from shore. Bald Eagle and Osprey visit here too. These species represent but a fraction of the birds present in and around the marsh.

Enjoy the view of Belgrade Bog from the public landing on Messalonskee Lake.

About this site

Set up a scope by the public boat launch (hand-carry only) parking area. This will enable you to scan a great portion of the bog. You can also get a good view of the bog and also the stream by sitting on the rocks along the stream crossing on Route 27, just slightly past the boat launch. Binoculars will serve well in spring, when waterfowl are nesting and are very much in evidence.

A canoe will give you a much better opportunity to view any number of species, no matter when you visit. A dock facilitates launching a canoe here; you can tie the canoe to the dock and load your gear with ease. Plan to spend at least half a day canoeing the stream and the lake's shoreline. If you go by canoe, you may also want to bring a camera, since you are liable to see so many desirable bird species. Also bring sunscreen and insect repellent.

Nearby opportunities

Belgrade Peninsula Park, behind Day's Store in Belgrade Lakes, is a prime viewing place for Bald Eagle in winter. Beaver and other carcasses are placed on the ice to provide food for eagles. Chances of seeing several eagles at once are good. The park has picnic tables to sit on, snow and ice conditions permitting.

Standing on the end of the peninsula and looking north, you may be able to discern eagle nests in some of the tall white pine trees lining the shore.

The park is only a few hundred feet from the famed spillway, a place where anglers typically catch huge brown trout in spring and fall. A birding/fishing visit to Belgrade Bog and the spillway at Belgrade Lakes can easily fill a day with excitement and fond memories. *DeLorme: Maine Atlas and Gazetteer:* Page 20, E4

Northern Maine

Northern Maine is at once the last and largest wild, undeveloped area in the eastern United States. But this region of spruce-fir forests and sphagnum bogs is far from a trackless wilderness. It is a place of commercial timberlands, and timber companies maintain the largest network of unpaved roads in the state, probably the northeast. Boreal species attract birders here. Waterfowl are thick on the region's lakes and ponds. Northern Maine is typified by the mournful cry of the Common Loon, something many people consider the true call of the wild.

Northern Maine

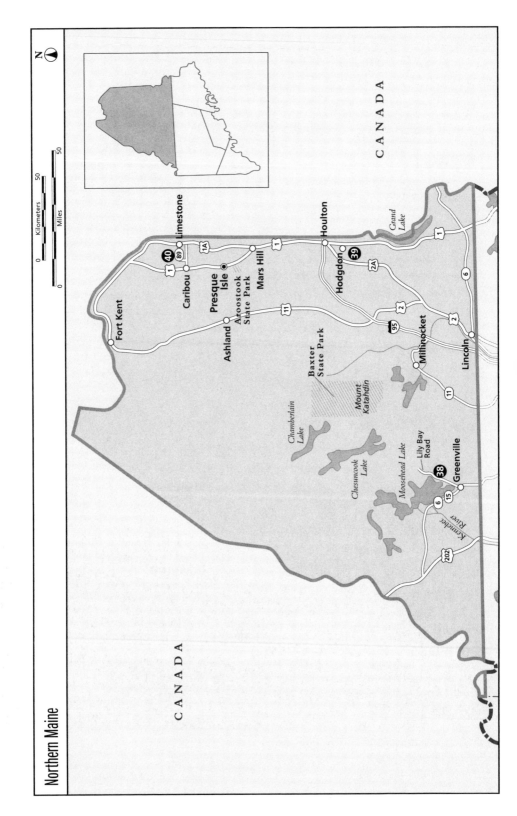

38 Lily Bay State Park

Habitats: Maine's largest freshwater lake, spruce-fir forest, and low growth along riparian habitat.

Best time to bird: Summer is best. Try to visit anytime from June through September.

Nearest gas, food, and lodging: Greenville has gas stations and plenty of restaurants, motels, lodges, and inns.

Nearest camping: Lily Bay State Park; (207) 695-2700 or (207) 941-4014; www.camp withme.com.

For more information: Lily Bay State Park, 13 Myrle's Way, Greenville, ME 04441; (207) 695-2700 (May through October) or (207) 941-4014 (November through April); www .campwithme.com.

Directions: From Greenville drive north on Lily Bay Road, for 9 miles. Look for a large wooden sign for Lily Bay State Park on the left. *DeLorme: Maine Atlas and Gazetteer:* Page 41, C3

Lily Bay State Park, one of the jewels of Maine's Moosehead Lake Region, is a favorite camping site for visiting birders.

The birds

Boreal species are key at Lily Bay State Park. The park and surrounding woodlands hosts Gray Jay, Boreal Chickadee, Spruce Grouse, and Black-backed Woodpecker. Additional species of interest sometimes seen around the park include Pileated Woodpecker, Yellow-bellied Sapsucker, and Rusty Blackbird. And, of course, Common Loon inhabit Moosehead Lake. These are easily viewed from shore, and their nighttime calls figure prominently in the overall experience of spending time in Maine's north woods.

For best chances of seeing a Spruce Grouse, look for the birds in trees. Don't expect a noisy flush as you walk through the woods, as with a Ruffed Grouse. Spruce Grouse are unafraid and will simply hop up in a tree and stare at you.

About this site

Lily Bay State Park, a 925-acre parcel on the east side of Moosehead Lake, presents in brief what the surrounding country has to offer. This is the gateway to the larger North Maine Woods.

The park offers camping, hiking, boating, and, of course, birding. Campsites are spread out, and the crowding that often occurs at other parks rarely happens here. This is a great place to stay, spend time, and explore not only the park but also the surrounding area.

Nearby opportunities

Big Moose Mountain is worth a visit. From Greenville head north on Routes 6/15 for about 2 miles; look for a sign on the left for Big Moose Mountain, just past the Scott Paper Company buildings. Turn left here and drive 1 mile to the Big Moose Mountain trailhead on the right. Key birds here include Bicknell's Thrush, Swainson's Thrush, Yellow-bellied Flycatcher, Black-polled Warbler, and Boreal Chickadee.

39 Lt. Gordon Manuel Wildlife Management Area

Habitats: Upland forests, wetlands, fields, and successional vegetation.

Best time to bird: Beginning in mid- to late April (this may happen later, depending on when spring arrives in the North Country), American Woodcock return to this WMA. Mid-May and June are prime times for waterfowl viewing. Land-based birds will be evident throughout the summer, especially early in the morning, and October will see migrating waterfowl that stop on their way south to feed in the marsh.

Nearest gas, food, and lodging: Houlton has restaurants, motels, and bed-and-breakfasts; gas is available along U.S. Route 1.

Nearest camping: Aroostook State Park, 87 State Park Road, Presque Isle; (207) 768-8341.

For more information: Maine Department of Inland Fisheries and Wildlife, 284 State Street, 41 State House Station, Augusta, ME 04333-0041; (207) 287-8000; www.mefishwildlife.com.

For Aroostook State Park, contact Maine Bureau of Parks and Lands, 22 State House Station, Augusta, ME 04333; (207) 768-8341; www.campwithme.com.

Directions: Take exit 302 off Interstate 95 to Houlton, and drive about 6 miles south on US 1, also called the Calais Road. In Hodgdon take the first right-hand (west) turn onto Hodgdon Mills Road. Drive a short distance to the small town center of Hodgdon, and look for Horseback Road on the left (south side). This is an access road for Lt. Gordon Manuel WMA. *DeLorme: Maine Atlas and Gazetteer:* Page 53, B3

The birds

A variety of waterfowl frequent the Hodgdon Deadwater—a wide, shallow section of the Meduxnekeag River. Great Blue Heron and Osprey have been noted. American Woodcock use the successional habitat and fields, and a variety of songbirds are found in wooded sections. While none have yet been recorded, Bald Eagle most likely frequent the area. Osprey are visible in spring and summer. A more comprehensive bird list has yet to be developed, since birders have not thoroughly explored this WMA. It is a great untapped resource.

This site has potential for many valuable birds, too. For instance, Upland Sandpiper, a Maine threatened species, were once common throughout the state because of ongoing agricultural practices that maintained fields and pastures. Sadly, agriculture in Maine and elsewhere has declined and, with it, the habitat required by Upland Sandpiper. Still, Aroostook County has its share of Upland Sandpiper. Do the fields at Lt. Gordon Manuel WMA host breeding pairs of Upland Sandpiper? Perhaps so, but that's for the reader to discover. Part of the mystique of this site lies in the secrets it contains.

Lt. Gordon Manuel Wildlife Management Area, as seen from the small town of Hodgdon, contains a wide variety of habitats and, consequently, a good number of bird species.

About this site

This 6,482-acre WMA has several unimproved roads leading through it, as well as some hiking trails. Visitors can launch a canoe from the boat landing in Hodgdon and spend a leisurely half day paddling and scanning the surface and edges of the deadwater for birds.

Farmland adjacent to the WMA undoubtedly helps to attract grassland birds.

As with so many other WMAs, Lt. Gordon Manuel WMA is in a natural state, with no structures, paved roads, or facilities of any kind. This is a wild, untamed site, and visitors need to come prepared. Two must-have items for this site are a compass and a *Maine Atlas and Gazetteer* or other detailed map.

Nearby opportunities

Aroostook State Park, just south of Presque Isle, offers some decent birding, even in winter. That's when Dark-eyed Junco, Tree Swallow, and Snow Bunting may visit the park and nearby environs in the Presque Isle Region. (Even though the park is only officially open from May 15 through October 15, birders may walk in as long as they don't block any roads.) Pileated Woodpecker are a possibility any time. In summer look for Common Loon, Canada Goose, several species of ducks, and Osprey. The 577-acre park contains a double-peaked mountain, forests, and a small lake stocked with brook trout.

To reach Aroostook State Park from Hodgdon Mills Road and US 1 in Hodgdon, drive north on US 1 to Presque Isle, about 42 miles. Look for Spragueville Road on the left (west) side of the road and a sign for Aroostook State Park. *DeLorme: Maine Atlas and Gazetteer:* Page 65, E1

(40) Aroostook National Wildlife Refuge

Habitats: Forested uplands, wetlands, and grasslands.

Best time to bird: Spring brings a wave of migrant warblers. These are evident in mid- and late May and into early summer. Nesting waterfowl are also abundant at this time. In early spring, which means mid- to late April and early May in Aroostook County, American Woodcock arrive. Fall, which begins in early September, sees waterfowl congregating prior to migration, which continues though October.

Access: Until the proposed autoroute is completed, access is limited to walking. No great physical difficulty is required, however.

Nearest gas, food, and lodging: Food and lodging are available in Limestone. Gas is available off Interstate 95 and along U.S. Route 1.

Nearest camping: Malabeam Campground, Limestone; (207) 328-4643. Trafton Lake Campground, Limestone; (207) 328-4025. Aroostook State Park, 87 State Park Road, Presque Isle; (207) 768-8341. Arndt's Aroostook River Lodge and Campground, Presque Isle; (207) 764-8677.

For more information: Aroostook National Wildlife Refuge, 97 Refuge Road, Limestone, ME 04760; (207) 328-4634; e-mail fw5rwmhnwr@fws.gov. See *Hiking Maine* (The Globe Pequot Press, 2002) for information on Aroostook State Park, and check *Maine Off the Beaten Path* (The Globe Pequot Press, 2006) for more information on the Limestone Region.

Directions: From Bangor drive north on I- 95 to Houlton, exit 302. Turn left, heading north on US 1 to Caribou. In Caribou turn right and head east on Route 89 toward Limestone. In Limestone turn left onto Loring Commerce Road; travel north for 2 miles to where the road crosses a set of railroad tracks. Cross the tracks and bear right (east) where the road forks, just past the tracks. Look for the refuge office and visitor contact station on the right. *DeLorme: Maine Atlas and Gazetteer:* Page 65, A3

The birds

The refuge's upland areas provide nesting habitat for warblers such as Black-throated Green, Canada, Bay-breasted, Cape May, and Blackburnian Warbler. Boreal Chickadee and Gray Jay are also fairly common in upland woods here, as are Ruffed Grouse. American Black Duck, Wood Duck, Hooded Merganser, Ring-necked Duck, Canada Goose, Bald Eagle, Great Blue Heron, and Belted Kingfisher frequent refuge wetlands. Upland Sandpiper, Bobolink, and Savannah Sparrow find suitable habitat on refuge grasslands. Unfortunately the grasslands are currently out of bounds to the public, but plans are in place for an autoroute through the grassland. No specific time has been set for this, however. Local experts sometimes lead bird walks at the refuge. Check with refuge headquarters for more information.

Mallard Duck are just one of the many species of waterfowl and other birds that visit Aroostook National Wildlife Refuge.

About this site

In 1998 the U.S. Air Force transferred 4,700 acres of the former Loring Air Force Base to the U.S. Fish and Wildlife Service. This became the Aroostook National Wildlife Refuge. The U.S. Fish and Wildlife Service actively manages the land to benefit wildlife. This includes removing man-made structures, roads, and fences. Additionally, controlled burns consume old vegetation, making way for new growth on refuge grasslands. Ongoing wetland restoration benefits birds as well as other kinds of wildlife.

While the refuge is here to stay, the future of the staffing is uncertain due to budget constraints. Also, funding cuts may limit the growth of habitat restoration. That said, the refuge remains open to visitors, and the vast potential for birding remains the same as always. When visiting the refuge, be sure to pick up a trail map at the headquarters.

Nearby opportunities

Another small but excellent spot for some quick birding is the Caribou Dam. The dam, which spans the Aroostook River in Caribou, presents an opportunity to see some interesting waterfowl. In late summer look for Great Blue Heron and Black-crowned Night Heron along the riparian habitat. In winter look for Common Merganser and Common Goldeneye on the water. Other possible wintertime birds include Iceland gull and Barrow's Goldeneye. *DeLorme: Maine Atlas and Gazetteer:* Page 65, B2

Appendix A: Maine Birding Information

The *Guillemot*

The Sorrento Scientific Society publishes its *Guillemot* newsletter every other month. The newsletter includes reported bird sightings from around Maine and coverage of the Christmas Bird Count, an annual event sponsored by the National Audubon Society. Also included are announcements for upcoming birding events, such as the Annual Down East Birding Festival at Cobscook Bay. A $5 contribution buys membership in the society and a year's subscription to *Guillemot*. There are no meetings of the society, only the newsletter. However, readers are invited to post their sightings. To post a sighting write to *Guillemot,* Newsletter of Sorrento Scientific Society, 12 Spring Street, Bar Harbor, ME 03609, call (207) 288-5654, or e-mail nature.reports@verizon.net. To subscribe send a check to the above address.

Maine Audubon

Maine Audubon, an affiliate of the National Audubon Society, has seven Maine chapters. Maine Audubon Headquarters are at Gilsland Farm Audubon Center, 20 Gilsland Farm Road, Falmouth, ME 04105; (207) 781-2330; www.maineaudubon.org.

Appendix B: Official Checklist of Maine Birds

The Maine Bird Records Committee considers the following 423 species to be positively documented within the state of Maine. The names and taxonomic arrangement follow the American Ornithologists' Union *Check-list* (seventh edition, 1998), as amended through its 45th supplement (*The Auk* 121: 985–995, 2003). This list was compiled through November 30, 2005, by the Maine Bird Records Committee: Peter Vickery (chair), Dennis Abbott, Louis Bevier, Lysle Brinker, Jody Despres, Scott Hall, Thomas Hodgman, Don Mairs, Jan Pierson, and Bill Sheehan (secretary). According to the committee's report:

Hypothetical species. Significant reports for 20 additional species exist for Maine. Although some probably are correct, the committee remains uncertain because we lack conclusive evidence at this time. We plan to review these species in the near future. The Maine Bird Records Committee defines a species in Maine as hypothetical if the record is thought to be accurate but the supporting documentation is not sufficiently complete to be accepted as a full record. Records in this category usually lack physical documentation, whether by specimen, photograph, or recording, or involve descriptions that are only partially adequate. Uncertainty regarding provenance or accuracy of locality information may also constitute reasons for placing a species on this list: *Barnacle Goose, Trumpeter Swan, Labrador Duck (extinct), Greater Prairie-Chicken (Heath Hen extinct), Northern Bobwhite, Black-browed Albatross, Cape Petrel, Black-capped Petrel, Audubon's Shearwater, Band-rumped Storm-Petrel, Thayer's Gull, Tufted Puffin, Vermilion Flycatcher, Gray Kingbird, Plumbeous Vireo, Black-billed Magpie, Eurasian Jackdaw, Bewick's Wren, Sprague's Pipit,* and *Boat-tailed Grackle.*

Failed species. The following introduced species bred for some years in Maine but never became established: *Gray Partridge* and *Monk Parakeet.*

Legend

*****: *Rare* (species name italicized): Written descriptions and, if possible, photographs and/or audio recordings should be submitted for any occurrence of these species in the state. Please send all reports to: Bill Sheehan, 1125 Woodland Center Road, Woodland, ME 04736 (e-mail me-brc@maine.rr.com), or Peter Vickery, Center for Ecological Research, P.O. Box 127, Richmond, ME 04357 (e-mail peter vickery@adelphia.net).

B: Breeds regularly

rb: Rare, very local, or less than annual breeder

ib: irregular breeder, only one or two isolated records

xb: No recent breeding; over twenty years since last breeding

NOTE: Reports of breeding by any species that is an irregular breeder (ib), that bred historically (xb), or that is not listed as having bred in Maine should be documented. Please send information to the addresses above.

N1: Introduced and established breeding population

N2: Populations successfully reestablished and breeding in areas of former occurrence

N3: Domesticated species with feral populations established and breeding in the wild

†: Extinct

Swans, Geese, & Ducks
- ❑ *Fulvous Whistling-Duck*
- ❑ Greater White-fronted Goose
- ❑ Snow Goose
- ❑ *Ross's Goose*
- ❑ Brant
- ❑ *Cackling Goose*
- ❑ Canada Goose B-N1
- ❑ Mute Swan rb-N1
- ❑ Tundra Swan
- ❑ *Whooper Swan*
- ❑ Wood Duck B
- ❑ Gadwall rb
- ❑ Eurasian Wigeon
- ❑ American Wigeon rb
- ❑ American Black Duck B
- ❑ Mallard B-N1
- ❑ Blue-winged Teal B
- ❑ Northern Shoveler rb
- ❑ Northern Pintail ib
- ❑ *Garganey*
- ❑ Green-winged Teal B
- ❑ Canvasback
- ❑ Redhead
- ❑ Ring-necked Duck B
- ❑ *Tufted Duck*
- ❑ Greater Scaup
- ❑ Lesser Scaup ib
- ❑ *Steller's Eider*
- ❑ King Eider
- ❑ Common Eider B
- ❑ Harlequin Duck
- ❑ Surf Scoter
- ❑ White-winged Scoter
- ❑ Black Scoter
- ❑ Long-tailed Duck
- ❑ Bufflehead
- ❑ Common Goldeneye B
- ❑ Barrow's Goldeneye
- ❑ Hooded Merganser B
- ❑ Common Merganser B
- ❑ Red-breasted Merganser B
- ❑ Ruddy Duck ib

Pheasants, Grouse, & Turkey
- ❑ Ring-necked Pheasant N1
- ❑ Ruffed Grouse B
- ❑ Spruce Grouse B
- ❑ *Willow Ptarmigan*
- ❑ Wild Turkey N2

Loons
- ❑ Red-throated Loon
- ❑ *Pacific Loon*
- ❑ Common Loon B

Grebes
- ❑ Pied-billed Grebe B
- ❑ Horned Grebe
- ❑ Red-necked Grebe
- ❑ *Eared Grebe*

❏ *Western Grebe
❏ *Clark's Grebe

Albatrosses
❏ *Yellow-nosed Albatross

Shearwaters
❏ Northern Fulmar
❏ Cory's Shearwater
❏ Greater Shearwater
❏ Sooty Shearwater
❏ Manx Shearwater

Storm-Petrels
❏ Wilson's Storm-Petrel
❏ Leach's Storm-Petrel B

Tropicbirds
❏ *White-tailed Tropicbird
❏ *Red-billed Tropicbird

Gannets & Boobies
❏ Northern Gannet

Pelicans
❏ *American White Pelican
❏ *Brown Pelican

Cormorants
❏ Double-crested Cormorant B
❏ Great Cormorant rb

Frigatebirds
❏ *Magnificent Frigatebird
❏ *Lesser Frigatebird

Bitterns, Herons, & Ibises
❏ American Bittern B
❏ Least Bittern B
❏ Great Blue Heron B
❏ Great Egret rb
❏ Snowy Egret B
❏ Little Blue Heron rb
❏ Tricolored Heron rb
❏ Cattle Egret rb
❏ Green Heron B
❏ Black-crowned Night-Heron B

❏ Yellow-crowned Night-Heron ib
❏ *White Ibis
❏ Glossy Ibis B
❏ *White-faced Ibis

Storks
❏ *Wood Stork

American Vultures
❏ * Black Vulture
❏ Turkey Vulture B

Kites, Eagles, & Hawks
❏ Osprey B
❏ *Swallow-tailed Kite
❏ *Mississippi Kite
❏ Bald Eagle B
❏ Northern Harrier B
❏ Sharp-shinned Hawk B
❏ Cooper's Hawk B
❏ Northern Goshawk B
❏ Red-shouldered Hawk B
❏ Broad-winged Hawk B
❏ *Swainson's Hawk
❏ Red-tailed Hawk B
❏ Rough-legged Hawk
❏ *Golden Eagle rb

Falcons
❏ American Kestrel B
❏ Merlin B
❏ Gyrfalcon
❏ Peregrine Falcon rb-N2

Rails, Gallinules, & Coots
❏ *Yellow Rail
❏ *Corn Crake
❏ *Clapper Rail
❏ *King Rail ib
❏ Virginia Rail B
❏ Sora B
❏ *Purple Gallinule
❏ Common Moorhen rb
❏ American Coot rb

Cranes
- [ ] Sandhill Crane rb

Plovers
- [ ] *Northern Lapwing*
- [ ] Black-bellied Plover
- [ ] American Golden-Plover
- [ ] *Pacific Golden-Plover*
- [ ] *Wilson's Plover*
- [ ] *Common Ringed Plover*
- [ ] Semipalmated Plover
- [ ] Piping Plover B
- [ ] Killdeer B

Oystercatchers
- [ ] American Oystercatcher rb

Stilts & Avocets
- [ ] *Black-necked Stilt*
- [ ] American Avocet

Sandpipers & Phalaropes
- [ ] Greater Yellowlegs
- [ ] Lesser Yellowlegs
- [ ] Solitary Sandpiper
- [ ] Willet B
- [ ] Spotted Sandpiper B
- [ ] Upland Sandpiper B
- [ ] † *Eskimo Curlew*
- [ ] Whimbrel
- [ ] *Long-billed Curlew*
- [ ] Hudsonian Godwit
- [ ] *Bar-tailed Godwit*
- [ ] Marbled Godwit
- [ ] Ruddy Turnstone
- [ ] Red Knot
- [ ] Sanderling
- [ ] Semipalmated Sandpiper
- [ ] Western Sandpiper
- [ ] *Red-necked Stint*
- [ ] Least Sandpiper
- [ ] White-rumped Sandpiper
- [ ] Baird's Sandpiper
- [ ] Pectoral Sandpiper

- [ ] Purple Sandpiper
- [ ] Dunlin
- [ ] *Curlew Sandpiper*
- [ ] Stilt Sandpiper
- [ ] Buff-breasted Sandpiper
- [ ] Ruff
- [ ] Short-billed Dowitcher
- [ ] Long-billed Dowitcher
- [ ] Wilson's Snipe B
- [ ] American Woodcock B
- [ ] Wilson's Phalarope ib
- [ ] Red-necked Phalarope
- [ ] Red Phalarope

Skuas, Gulls, Terns, & Skimmers
- [ ] Great Skua
- [ ] *South Polar Skua*
- [ ] Pomarine Jaeger
- [ ] Parasitic Jaeger
- [ ] *Long-tailed Jaeger*
- [ ] Laughing Gull B
- [ ] *Franklin's Gull*
- [ ] Little Gull
- [ ] Black-headed Gull rb
- [ ] Bonaparte's Gull rb
- [ ] *Mew Gull*
- [ ] Ring-billed Gull B
- [ ] Herring Gull B
- [ ] Iceland Gull
- [ ] Lesser Black-backed Gull
- [ ] Glaucous Gull
- [ ] Great Black-backed Gull B
- [ ] *Sabine's Gull*
- [ ] Black-legged Kittiwake
- [ ] *Ivory Gull*
- [ ] *Gull-billed Tern*
- [ ] Caspian Tern
- [ ] Royal Tern
- [ ] *Sandwich Tern*
- [ ] Roseate Tern B
- [ ] Common Tern B
- [ ] Arctic Tern B

❏ Forster's Tern
❏ Least Tern B
❏ *Bridled Tern*
❏ *Sooty Tern*
❏ *White-winged Tern*
❏ Black Tern B
❏ *Black Skimmer*

Auks, Murres, & Puffins
❏ Dovekie
❏ Common Murre xb
❏ Thick-billed Murre
❏ Razorbill B
❏ † *Great Auk xb*
❏ Black Guillemot B
❏ Atlantic Puffin B

Pigeons & Doves
❏ Rock Pigeon N3
❏ *Band-tailed Pigeon*
❏ *White-winged Dove*
❏ Mourning Dove B
❏ † *Passenger Pigeon xb*

Cuckoos
❏ Black-billed Cuckoo B
❏ Yellow-billed Cuckoo B

Barn Owls
❏ *Barn Owl xb*

Typical Owls
❏ *Eastern Screech-Owl xb*
❏ Great Horned Owl B
❏ Snowy Owl
❏ Northern Hawk Owl
❏ Barred Owl B
❏ Great Gray Owl
❏ Long-eared Owl rb
❏ Short-eared Owl ib
❏ Boreal Owl
❏ Northern Saw-whet Owl B

Goatsuckers
❏ Common Nighthawk B
❏ *Chuck-will's-widow*
❏ Whip-poor-will B

Swifts
❏ Chimney Swift B

Hummingbirds
❏ Ruby-throated Hummingbird B
❏ *Calliope Hummingbird*
❏ *Rufous Hummingbird*

Kingfishers
❏ Belted Kingfisher B

Woodpeckers
❏ Red-headed Woodpecker xb
❏ Red-bellied Woodpecker ib
❏ Yellow-bellied Sapsucker B
❏ Downy Woodpecker B
❏ Hairy Woodpecker B
❏ American Three-toed Wood-pecker rb
❏ Black-backed Woodpecker B
❏ Northern Flicker B
❏ Pileated Woodpecker B

Tyrant Flycatchers
❏ Olive-sided Flycatcher B
❏ Eastern Wood-Pewee B
❏ Yellow-bellied Flycatcher B
❏ Acadian Flycatcher
❏ Alder Flycatcher B
❏ Willow Flycatcher B
❏ Least Flycatcher B
❏ Eastern Phoebe B
❏ *Say's Phoebe*
❏ *Ash-throated Flycatcher*
❏ Great Crested Flycatcher B
❏ *Variegated Flycatcher*
❏ *Tropical Kingbird*
❏ Western Kingbird
❏ Eastern Kingbird B

❏ Scissor-tailed Flycatcher ib
❏ *Fork-tailed Flycatcher*

Shrikes
❏ *Loggerhead Shrike xb*
❏ Northern Shrike

Vireos
❏ White-eyed Vireo
❏ *Bell's Vireo*
❏ Yellow-throated Vireo B
❏ Blue-headed Vireo B
❏ Warbling Vireo B
❏ Philadelphia Vireo B
❏ Red-eyed Vireo B

Jays & Crows
❏ Gray Jay B
❏ Blue Jay B
❏ American Crow B
❏ Fish Crow rb
❏ Common Raven B

Larks
❏ Horned Lark B

Swallows
❏ Purple Martin B
❏ Tree Swallow B
❏ Northern Rough-winged Swallow B
❏ Bank Swallow B
❏ Cliff Swallow B
❏ *Cave Swallow*
❏ Barn Swallow B

Chickadees & Titmice
❏ Black-capped Chickadee B
❏ Boreal Chickadee B
❏ Tufted Titmouse B

Nuthatches
❏ Red-breasted Nuthatch B
❏ White-breasted Nuthatch B

Creepers
❏ Brown Creeper B

Wrens
❏ Carolina Wren rb
❏ House Wren B
❏ Winter Wren B
❏ *Sedge Wren rb*
❏ Marsh Wren B

Kinglets
❏ Golden-crowned Kinglet B
❏ Ruby-crowned Kinglet B

Gnatcatchers
❏ Blue-gray Gnatcatcher B

Thrushes
❏ Northern Wheatear
❏ Eastern Bluebird B
❏ *Townsend's Solitaire*
❏ Veery B
❏ Gray-cheeked Thrush
❏ Bicknell's Thrush B
❏ Swainson's Thrush B
❏ Hermit Thrush B
❏ Wood Thrush B
❏ American Robin B
❏ Varied Thrush

Mockingbirds & Thrashers
❏ Gray Catbird B
❏ Northern Mockingbird B
❏ *Sage Thrasher*
❏ Brown Thrasher B

Starlings
❏ European Starling N1

Pipits
❏ American Pipit rb

Waxwings
❏ Bohemian Waxwing
❏ Cedar Waxwing B

Wood-Warblers

- ❏ Blue-winged Warbler B
- ❏ Golden-winged Warbler
- ❏ Tennessee Warbler B
- ❏ Orange-crowned Warbler
- ❏ Nashville Warbler B
- ❏ *Virginia's Warbler*
- ❏ Northern Parula B
- ❏ Yellow Warbler B
- ❏ Chestnut-sided Warbler B
- ❏ Magnolia Warbler B
- ❏ Cape May Warbler B
- ❏ Black-throated Blue Warbler B
- ❏ Yellow-rumped Warbler B
- ❏ *Black-throated Gray Warbler*
- ❏ Black-throated Green Warbler B
- ❏ *Townsend's Warbler*
- ❏ Blackburnian Warbler B
- ❏ Yellow-throated Warbler
- ❏ Pine Warbler B
- ❏ Prairie Warbler B
- ❏ Palm Warbler B
- ❏ Bay-breasted Warbler B
- ❏ Blackpoll Warbler B
- ❏ Cerulean Warbler
- ❏ Black-and-white Warbler B
- ❏ American Redstart B
- ❏ Prothonotary Warbler
- ❏ Worm-eating Warbler
- ❏ *Swainson's Warbler*
- ❏ Ovenbird B
- ❏ Northern Waterthrush B
- ❏ Louisiana Waterthrush B
- ❏ Kentucky Warbler
- ❏ Connecticut Warbler
- ❏ Mourning Warbler B
- ❏ Common Yellowthroat B
- ❏ Hooded Warbler
- ❏ Wilson's Warbler B
- ❏ Canada Warbler B
- ❏ Yellow-breasted Chat

Tanagers

- ❏ Summer Tanager
- ❏ Scarlet Tanager B
- ❏ *Western Tanager*

Towhees, Sparrows, & Longspurs

- ❏ *Green-tailed Towhee*
- ❏ Eastern Towhee B
- ❏ *Cassin's Sparrow*
- ❏ American Tree Sparrow
- ❏ Chipping Sparrow B
- ❏ Clay-colored Sparrow ib
- ❏ Field Sparrow B
- ❏ Vesper Sparrow B
- ❏ Lark Sparrow
- ❏ *Black-throated Sparrow*
- ❏ *Lark Bunting*
- ❏ Savannah Sparrow B
- ❏ Grasshopper Sparrow rb
- ❏ *Henslow's Sparrow*
- ❏ *Le Conte's Sparrow*
- ❏ Nelson's Sharp-tailed Sparrow B
- ❏ Saltmarsh Sharp-tailed Sparrow B
- ❏ Seaside Sparrow ib
- ❏ Fox Sparrow ib
- ❏ Song Sparrow B
- ❏ Lincoln's Sparrow B
- ❏ Swamp Sparrow B
- ❏ White-throated Sparrow B
- ❏ *Harris's Sparrow*
- ❏ White-crowned Sparrow
- ❏ *Golden-crowned Sparrow*
- ❏ Dark-eyed Junco B
- ❏ Lapland Longspur
- ❏ *Smith's Longspur*
- ❏ *Chestnut-collared Longspur*
- ❏ Snow Bunting

Cardinals, Grosbeaks, & Buntings

- ❏ Northern Cardinal B
- ❏ Rose-breasted Grosbeak B
- ❏ *Black-headed Grosbeak*
- ❏ Blue Grosbeak

- ❏ *Lazuli Bunting*
- ❏ Indigo Bunting B
- ❏ *Painted Bunting*
- ❏ Dickcissel

Blackbirds & Orioles
- ❏ Bobolink B
- ❏ Red-winged Blackbird B
- ❏ Eastern Meadowlark B
- ❏ *Western Meadowlark*
- ❏ Yellow-headed Blackbird
- ❏ Rusty Blackbird rb
- ❏ *Brewer's Blackbird*
- ❏ Common Grackle B
- ❏ *Shiny Cowbird*
- ❏ Brown-headed Cowbird B
- ❏ Orchard Oriole rb
- ❏ *Bullock's Oriole*
- ❏ Baltimore Oriole B

Finches
- ❏ *Common Chaffinch*
- ❏ *Gray-crowned Rosy-Finch*
- ❏ Pine Grosbeak ib
- ❏ Purple Finch B
- ❏ House Finch N1
- ❏ Red Crossbill B
- ❏ White-winged Crossbill B
- ❏ Common Redpoll
- ❏ Hoary Redpoll
- ❏ *Eurasian Siskin*
- ❏ Pine Siskin B
- ❏ *Lesser Goldfinch*
- ❏ American Goldfinch B
- ❏ Evening Grosbeak B

Old World Sparrows
- ❏ House Sparrow N1

About the Author

Tom Seymour, a freelance writer and longtime columnist for the *Maine Sportsman* magazine and the *Republican Journal*, Belfast, Maine's weekly newspaper, loves to fish. Since Tom covers the Down East, Midcoast, and Moosehead Lake regions for the *Maine Sportsman,* much of his time is spent fishing around and about Maine.

Tom has authored *Fishing Maine, Hiking Maine,* and *Foraging New England* and has revised and edited *Maine Off the Beaten Path* for The Globe Pequot Press. *Tom Seymour's Maine, a Maine Anthology,* published by iUniverse, Inc., has become a regional favorite with its chapters on Maine history and folklore, highlighted by firsthand accounts of trips through the Maine wilderness on the Canada Road and tales of the British invasion of Belfast. In 2006 the *Maine Sportsman* put a collection of Tom's "Maine Wildlife" columns into book form as an inducement to subscribers. *Maine Wildlife, Up-Close and Personal Encounters of a Maine Naturalist,* is filled with accounts of Tom's personal experience with Maine wildlife.

When not fishing or playing the Highland bagpipes or Scottish smallpipes, Tom can be found leading nature walks for folks seeking to learn more about wild edible plants.